STUDIES IN SOCIOLOGY

Consulting Editor:

CHARLES H. PAGE

University of Massachusetts

CELIA S. HELLER

Hunter College

Mexican American Youth

Forgotten Youth at the Crossroads

RANDOM HOUSE

NEW YORK

[ACKNOWLEDGMENTS]

The names of all those who directly or indirectly have helped to make this book possible would make a very long list. I acknowledge with pleasure my special indebtedness to the following people: to Elisabeth Frank for arousing my interest in Mexican Americans; to Ralph H. Turner for his generosity in making available to me certain materials that he collected; to Donald R. Cressey for encouraging me to continue my study of juvenile offenses among Mexican Americans; to Ralph Beals for his advice and kindness; and to Charles Page for his criticism of the manuscript and editorial aid. I also wish to thank the National Institute of Mental Health and the Ford Foundation for their financial awards.

[CONTENTS]

[ONE]

Introduction

The Mexican American minority has received little attention from the mass media of communication and, outside the Southwest, there is hardly any awareness of its existence. This merits some thought, especially since the Mexican Americans are the third largest minority in the United States.[1] Moreover, in those southwestern states, where they are concentrated, an awareness exists but there is no corresponding knowledge about them. Of course, few people in those states would admit ignorance, and more would vouch that they "know all there is to know" about Mexican Americans. The "all" very often consists of a stereotypic image of Mexican Americans that is widespread. I have heard numerous comments which reflect it. The comments about Mexican American youth in particular—made even by individuals having contact with them, such as teachers, school administrators, and social workers—run something like this: How "Mexican" the young people are in their ways, how lacking in ambition, how prone to delinquent behavior.

Even for the person who is not satisfied with those stereotypes it is not easy to obtain factual knowledge. The meager literature about the Mexican Americans both reflects and contributes to their being unremembered and little known. Not much of a systematic nature has been written about Mexican Americans today, particularly about Mexican American youth. As a matter of fact, there seems to be a general agreement among interested social scientists that the field of Mexican American studies has been sadly neglected from the forties to the present day, although it did attract the attention of social scientists in earlier years.

The present study is an attempt to fill, if only partially, this gap. It concentrates on the Mexican American youth. Besides the apparent reasons for singling out the youth for study, they provide us with the opportunity of exploring whether or not new trends are appearing among Mexican Americans. Such exploration gains in importance when viewed from the perspective of the following facts, which will be elaborated in this book. Both in the rate and the degree of acculturation and assimilation Mexican Americans are among the least "Americanized" of all ethnic groups in the United States. Their educational and occupational achievements have been consistently limited. In these and other socioeconomic characteristics they rank "close to lowest" among all minority groups.[2] As compared with most of them, they display a marked lack of internal differentiation, whether in terms of schooling, occupation, or income.[3] But perhaps more striking yet is the conclusion arrived at by Donald J. Bogue on the basis of his careful analysis of the 1950 Census data, that *of all ethnic groups in the United States, the Mexican Americans constitute "the only ethnic group for which a comparison of the characteristics of the first and second generation fails to show a substantial intergenerational rise in socio-economic status"* (italics supplied).[4] And just as there is very little intergenerational vertical mobility, so too there is no appreciable intergenerational geographic mobility.[5]

The scope of this book is the male Mexican American youth population in general. Although it focuses some attention on two polar types—the "ambitious boys" and the "delinquent boys"—it does so not only for the purpose of understanding them but also to gain insight into the problems of Mexican American youth as a whole. Each of these extreme segments is approached from the viewpoint of the characteristic which differentiates it most from the rest of Mexican American youth. In the case of the first it is its pattern of mobility aspirations and in the case of the second it is its pattern of offenses that provide the central themes. It is important that the delinquent segment be examined objectively because Mexican American youth is often equated with it. But more salient is the study of the first segment because it yields knowledge regarding the young people from whom will probably emerge not only the Mexican American future leadership but also the "models of success" for some future generations. Because they will provide the leadership and the models, it is especially important to know their ambitions and their values as well as their difficulties.

Due to the paucity of systematic studies about Mexican Americans much that is said in this book is tentative and awaits further validation. The book relies heavily on my own two quantitative studies of Los Angeles Mexican American youth, depth interviews, and field notes. However, the findings of these studies and of a number of recent doctoral dissertations are presented and interpreted within the context of the available published literature on Mexican Americans.

Extensively utilized in this study are the 1960 Census data which, to the best of my knowledge, have not been used before in published writings about Mexican Americans. They are of considerable importance because they constitute both the most recent and the most rigorous data about the Mexican American group as a whole. The original figures on which our calculations are based appear in a separate report, released in 1963, on the population with Spanish surname in the five states where the overwhelming majority of Mexican Americans concentrate.*

The type of analysis pursued throughout the book—whether it utilizes qualitative or quantitative materials, systematic data or more casual observations—is essentially comparative. The Mexican American youth is at times explicitly and often implicitly compared with the majority youth, and occasionally with the youth of other minority groups.

A few words are in order regarding the nomenclature used in reference to the minority group in this study and the majority group with which it is compared. This is not a trivial problem but one more seri-

---

* Although the figures do represent, according to experts, a fairly high approximation to the actual numbers of Mexican Americans, the data are limited. For example, they do include some individuals who are not Mexican American and fail to include some who are. To the first category belongs the small number of immigrants or descendants of immigrants from Spain and Latin American countries other than Mexico. To the latter belong those Mexican Americans who live outside these five states, Mexican American women who have intermarried, and those who have anglicized their names. Perhaps the two categories cancel each other out. (For details, see: "Definitions and Explanations," U. S. Census of Population, 1960: *Persons of Spanish Surname*, Final Report, PC(2)-1B, pp. VIII-XI; William W. Winnie, Jr., "The Spanish Surname Criterion for Identifying Hispanos in the Southwestern United States: A Preliminary Evaluation," *Social Forces*, 38 (May, 1960), pp. 363-6.)

ous than might appear at first. People of Mexican descent, as well as those born in Mexico, identify themselves with pride as members of *La Raza* (the Race), united by esoteric bonds of blood and custom. In a less serious vein, they call themselves *Chicanos*, a term which seems to have evolved in the United States. They also refer to themselves as "Mexicans" or "Mexicanos," but tend to resent these terms when applied to them by the majority population because of the derogatory connotations attached to these names. Thus it is considered more thoughtful and polite in the Southwest to speak of them as Spanish.[6] Since these people are not Spanish, some social scientists seem to have reached a compromise by referring to them as Spanish-speaking.[7] I consider this a misleading term, especially when studying people of Mexican origin, since among the Spanish-speaking people in the Southwest are some who hail from other Latin American countries. Their position, their reasons for being there, their history in the United States, and their socioeconomic conditions are often entirely different. When I explained these reservations to some Mexican Americans whom I came to know well, they told me that they considered it quite proper for outsiders to speak of "people of Mexican descent," but that they resented the hyphenated term "Mexican-American." Ruth Tuck seems to have responded to this resentment of the hyphenated term when she made the point and elaborated upon it with feeling that "the unqualified title American is very seldom used in regard to them."[8]

I tried the above solution—"people of Mexican descent"—but found the constant use of this longer expression rather cumbersome in writing. I am confident that I will be forgiven for using the term "Mexican American" (without the hyphen), inasmuch as I refer to the majority group as "Anglo American." (The term "Anglo" is widely used in the Southwest to designate nonforeign-born whites who are not of Mexican origin.) Also, the term "Mexican American" is now coming into wider usage among the youth of Mexican origin.

Notes

1. George E. Simpson and J. Milton Yinger, *Racial and Cultural Minorities*, New York: Harper, 1958, p. 811.

2. Charles F. Marden, *Minorities in American Society*, New York: American Book Co., 1952, p. 139.

3. Leonard Broom and Eshref Shevky, "Mexicans in the United States—A Problem of Social Differentiation," *Sociology and Social Research*, 36 (January-February, 1952), pp. 150-8.

4. Donald J. Bogue, *The Population of the United States*, Glencoe: The Free Press, 1959, p. 372.

5. E. P. Hutchinson, *Immigrants and Their Children*, New York: John Wiley, 1956, p. 59.

6. James B. Watson and Julian Samora, "Subordinate Leadership in a Bicultural Community: An Analysis," *American Sociological Review*, 19 (August, 1954), p. 420.

7. Muzafer Sherif and Carolyn W. Sherif, *Reference Groups —Exploration into Conformity and Deviation of Adolescents*, New York: Harper & Row, 1964, p. 169.

8. Ruth Tuck, *Not with the Fist*, New York: Harcourt, Brace, 1946, pp. xi-xii.

TWO

Origin and Background

Historical Profile

The Mexican American ethnic group, the third largest minority in the United States, is largely concentrated in the five southwestern states: Arizona, California, Colorado, New Mexico, and Texas. Over one tenth of the total population there is Mexican American, ranging from nine percent in Colorado and California to 28 percent in New Mexico. Of the 3,464,999 persons who, according to the 1960 Census, constitute the total population of Spanish surname in the Southwest, 2,844,-348 live in two states: California and Texas. Outside the Southwest, Mexican American communities are found in a number of cities, such as Chicago, Detroit, Gary, and Kansas City.

It is a fast growing group as evidenced by its 51 percent increase between 1950 and 1960, compared with

the 39 percent increase in the total population of the
five southwestern states. During this ten year period the
population of Spanish surname increased most in California, by 88 percent (compared with 49 percent for
the total population), and least in New Mexico, by
eight percent (compared with 40 percent of the total
population).[1]

It should not be forgotten that these areas originally
belonged to Mexico and came under the American flag
by the annexation of Texas, the Treaty of Guadalupe
Hidalgo, and the Gadsden Purchase. The Mexican past
is clearly reflected in the names of the mountains, riv-
ers, and towns of these states. In Carey McWilliams'
words the Mexicans "were very much part of the landscape when the Anglo Americans" came here.[2] And how
much the landscape of these states resembles that of
Mexico is clear to anyone who has visited both.

Some of the Mexican Americans today are the descendants of the people who lived in these territories
before they became part of the United States. They
predominate among the Mexican Americans of southern Colorado and northern New Mexico. A few villages
in these areas are still left intact, composed entirely of
such inhabitants.[3] For some of the descendants of the
original population, especially the wealthier ones, the
dominant group reserves the name Spanish-American,
Spanish-Colonial, or Hispano. These terms distinguish
them sharply—and they in turn tend to do the same
when in contact with the dominant group—from the
vast majority of Mexican Americans who are immigrants and children or grandchildren of immigrants
from Mexico.

These latter came from Mexico after 1900 as part of
the great wave of immigration. The Mexicans were un-
affected by the restrictive immigration laws of 1921
and 1924, which substantially reduced the supply of
labor from southeastern and eastern Europe.[4] They

entered the American labor market as common laborers and their employment—whether agricultural, for
example in the sugar beet fields, or industrial, as in
railroad maintenance—was largely periodic and migra-
tory. Then, too, there were large numbers of Mexican
"wetbacks" who had entered illegally. This illegal immigration reached unusual proportions in the post-
World War II period.[5]

Sometimes the *braceros* are erroneously thought of
as part of the Mexican American population. They
should be distinguished from the Mexican Americans,
since their stay in the United States was temporary and
seasonal. These agricultural workers, who had permits
to work as contract laborers for a specified period of
time, were brought to the United States by western
farmers under the seasonal labor importation statute,
Public Law 78. This statute was allowed to expire at
the end of 1964, and the *braceros* are now no longer
admitted to the United States.*

---

* Public Law 78 was passed in 1951 as a temporary emer-
gency measure to cope with reputed shortages of farm labor due
to the Korean War, and it was renewed periodically. (See: Arnold
Mayer, "The Grapes of Wrath, Vintage, 1961," *The Reporter*,
February 2, 1961, pp. 34-7). In May 1963 Congress voted against
an extension of the Mexican Contract Labor (Bracero Program),
but in December 1963 the program was extended for another
year. The program was allowed to expire on December 31, 1964.
It was terminated as a result of the position taken by representa-
tives of organized labor and welfare organizations and also by
some economists. They argued that this program tended to de-
press wages and working conditions and to increase domestic un-
employment. (See: Paul P. Kennedy, "Conference Sifts U. S.–
Mexico Issues—Two Nations' Lawmakers Hold 5th Annual
Reunion," *The New York Times*, February 21, 1965, 31:2.) This
source of agricultural labor was cut off despite the heated protests
of western farmers, who claimed that qualified domestic labor was
unavailable. They have fought since to reinstate the program.
After its expiration, at a hearing before the Senate Agricultural
Committee, spokesmen for western growers contended that there
was a labor shortage, but the Secretary of Labor, W. Willard
Wirtz, stated that, to the best of his knowledge, there was no

Although in the past Mexican Americans were largely agricultural workers, they have become increasingly urban in residence between 1920 and today.[6] The 1960 Census shows that the great bulk of them—about 80 percent, similar to the Anglo Americans in the Southwest—are found in urban areas (2,741,000 out of the total of 3,465,000).

Socioeconomic Characteristics

Thirty-five years ago Manuel Gamio, in his classical work on Mexicans in the United States, showed that, even if "they are American citizens, they remain on economic, political and social levels always inferior to those occupied by Americans of like condition and capacity." [7] This is still true today, as expressed in the 1960 Census data, even though 85 percent of the Mexican American population is native born. (More than half of the Mexican Americans have both parents born in the United States.)

Mexican Americans are found in all walks of life but there are relatively few in high-ranking and many in low-ranking occupations. (See Table 1.) Three fourths of Mexican Americans (76 percent), as compared with just over half (54 percent) of all employed "white" men in the United States, are manual workers. In the two opposite categories of the occupational scale, they are substantially underrepresented as professionals and overrepresented as laborers. Only five percent of the urban employed Mexican American males but 16 percent of the Anglo American males of the five southwestern states

---

shortage of qualified domestic labor. He maintained that any action by him to reinstate the program under existing conditions would be morally, economically, and legally wrong. (See: "Wirtz Denies U. S. Needs Braceros," *The New York Times*, January 16, 1965, 12:1.)

Table 1 OCCUPATIONAL DISTRIBUTION OF EMPLOYED URBAN MEXICAN AMERICAN MALES AND ANGLO AMERICAN MALES IN FIVE SOUTHWESTERN STATES: 1960* (in percentages)†

	Five States Total		Arizona		California		Colorado		New Mexico		Texas	
	Mexican American	Anglo American	Mexican American	Anglo American	Mexican American	Anglo American	Mexican American	Anglo American	Mexican American	Anglo American	Mexican American	Anglo American
Professional, technical, etc.	4.8	15.9	3.5	14.1	5.4	16.6	5.3	15.7	7.1	19.3	3.9	14.4
Farmers & farm managers	.7	.7	.4	.9	.8	.6	.1	.6	.5	.8	.6	1.0
Managers & proprietors, exc. farm	5.2	15.4	5.1	16.1	4.8	14.4	3.8	15.9	6.5	17.9	5.6	17.3
Clerical and kindred	5.8	8.2	3.7	6.9	5.8	8.2	5.7	8.5	8.5	6.7	5.8	8.5
Sales workers	4.2	9.7	3.8	10.0	3.9	9.5	3.6	9.4	4.7	7.8	4.7	10.1
Craftsmen, foremen, etc.	19.2	22.5	18.4	23.8	19.3	22.7	15.3	21.4	20.0	22.4	19.5	22.3
Operative, etc.	26.8	16.6	27.8	15.8	28.5	16.3	28.7	15.7	21.8	16.4	25.0	17.5
Private household workers	.1	.1	.1	.1	.1	.1	.1	.1	.1	.1	.1	.1
Service workers, exc. private household	8.8	5.7	8.2	5.9	7.7	6.1	11.4	6.4	13.5	4.5	9.5	4.2
Farm laborers & foremen	7.7	.6	10.5	1.0	8.9	.7	3.0	.6	1.7	.5	6.9	.5
Other laborers	16.7	4.6	18.4	5.3	14.8	4.8	23.0	5.7	15.6	3.6	18.5	4.1
TOTAL	100.0	100.0	100.0	100.0	100.0	100.0	100.0	100.0	100.0	100.0	100.0	100.0

SOURCES: U. S. Census of Population: 1960, Persons of Spanish Surname, Final Report PC(2)-1B, Table 6, p. 38, State volumes, Table 57.

* Mexican American stands for persons of Spanish surname, Anglo American for white persons, excluding those of Spanish surname.
† From the files of the Mexican-American Study Project, University of California, Los Angeles.

are in the professions. As many as 24 percent of the former but only five percent of the latter are laborers.

Concentration in unskilled occupations means of course that Mexican Americans characteristically earn much less than most other groups in the United States. Thus, in 1960, the median annual income of all wage and salary earners among the "white" segment of the U. S. population was slightly more than 3,000 dollars, while the comparable figure for Mexican Americans in the Southwest was close to 2,000 dollars; among urban males the earnings in the two groups were about 4,800 and 3,200 dollars, respectively. Income levels vary from state to state for most groups, with Mexican urban males showing (in 1960) a strong contrast between a median of about 4,180 dollars in California and about 2,300 dollars in Texas—the two extremes.

Inspection of *family* incomes in the Southwest indicates that more than twice as large a proportion of urban Mexican American families (31 percent) as Anglo American families (13 percent) earned less than 3,000 dollars in 1960. In Texas, where they fare worst among the five southwestern states, over one half of all Mexican American family incomes fell below the 3,000 figure.[8] And in California, where they fare best, and even in those of its counties where the Mexican Americans have the highest incomes, the incomes were substantially lower than those of the Anglo Americans. For example, in Los Angeles County the median family income for Mexican Americans was about 5,760 dollars and that for Anglo Americans 7,430 dollars.[9]

Consistent with their occupational and income position, the educational attainment of Mexican Americans also ranks substantially below that of the majority of the population. In 1960 the median number of school years completed was 8.1 years for Mexican American males (in urban areas 8.4), as compared with 10.3 (urban—11.0) of the total U. S. male population, 14 years old and over. It is noteworthy that the median for native-born Mexican American males, with both parents also native born, was only 8.6, but that of white native-born males of native parentage in general was 11 years of schooling. In the five southwestern states the median school years completed by Mexican American males ranged from a high of 8.9 years in California to a low of 6.2 in Texas.

If the comparison is limited to two extreme categories, a minimal education and a higher education, one finds Mexican Americans strikingly overrepresented in the former and underrepresented in the latter category. In the five southwestern states, more than one third (36 percent) of the Mexican American males but only five percent of the Anglo American males, 25 years of age and over, were illiterate (with no schooling) or functionally illiterate (having one to four years of schooling). If one shifts the analysis to males 14 years of age and over, the corresponding figure is still high for Mexican Americans: 29 percent as compared with six percent of all "white" males in the United States. Even among urban third (or later) generation Mexican American males in this age category—those with both parents native born—16 percent had less than five years of schooling. At the other end of the educational scale, as few as eight percent of Mexican American but 27 percent of Anglo American males, 25 years of age and over, in the Southwest had completed one or more years of college.[10]

There has been some comment in the sociological literature on the lack of internal differentiation among Mexican Americans as compared with most other ethnic groups, in terms of schooling, occupation, and income.[11] As suggested by the figures given above, this continues to be largely the case. Analysis of the 1960 Census figures shows the Mexican Americans to be an unusually homogeneous ethnic group. Whether native born or foreign born, whether of native or foreign parentage, whether urban or rural, they generally rank very low as measured by standard socioeconomic characteristics. (They do, however, differ in these characteristics along state lines: of the Mexican Americans in the five southwestern states, those in California rank highest and those in Texas rank lowest in occupation, education, and income.)

Social Stratification

This homogeneity in socioeconomic status seems to be mirrored in the thinking of Mexican Americans about their group, *La Raza*. The findings of a recent study suggest that many of this group have very little conception of internal socioeconomic differences. The study was conducted in Pomona, California, whose Mexican American community is in some ways atypical. It is more stable, more educated, and better housed than many other Mexican American communities in California, let alone in the other southwestern states. Yet even here, when questioned as to what the most important differences were among the Mexicans of Pomona, 42 percent of the sample of Mexican American adults in the city were unable to answer. Of those who did answer, two thirds did so in terms of socioeconomic status and one third in terms of acculturation.[12]

Notwithstanding this relative homogeneity, a number of studies nevertheless suggest that Mexican American communities in the Southwest are to some extent internally stratified. Most of them distinguish two social strata.[13] However, in his well-known investigation of the Tucson, Arizona, Mexican community, George Barker speaks of as many as five strata. In this community at the top are a few wealthy "old families" and below them wealthy families without distinguished ancestry. The middle layer consists of shopkeepers, clerks, and skilled workers. Below it are two strata: an "upper-lower" stratum of steadily employed unskilled and semiskilled workers, and a "lower-lower" stratum of unskilled migrant workers.[14] Fernando Penalosa, the author of the Pomona study cited above—one of the most thorough reports of the stratification system in a Mexican American community—contends that there are four strata, or what he calls "levels," among the Mexican Americans of Pomona. The lowest level consists of the poorest, least acculturated, and least skilled. The next, in which the majority of the Mexican Americans are located, is composed of steadily employed unskilled and semiskilled workers. Above them are those who have achieved a "modest degree of success": skilled workers earning about 8,000 dollars annually or more. Finally, there is the top level, which Penalosa considers "fully equivalent to the Anglo middle class." Its members tend to be described by the other Mexican Americans in the community as "society," but they refer to themselves as "middle class." Penalosa found in this group no descendants of "old families" (presumably there were no such families in Pomona). But he did find among them the most successful and most acculturated individuals of the Mexican American community. This and other considerations have led him to the conclusion that mobility and acculturation were two closely associated processes in this Mexican American community.[15]

Religion

The minimal acculturation and assimilation of the Mexican Americans, reflected in their socioeconomic status, are also manifested in their religious behavior. We are not referring only to the fact that to a large degree they have retained the Catholic affiliation of their forefathers. Figures showing the proportion

of Catholics in the entire Mexican American population are not available. However, a study of a specific
community, San Jose, California, cites the following
estimate of the religious distribution of its Mexican
American residents in 1955. Only 4 percent of them
had no church affiliation, 70 percent were Catholic,
and 26 percent were Protestant.[16] On the basis of casual
observation, one would guess that the percentage of
Protestants in the total Mexican American population
is not as high as in San Jose. There is, however, the
autonomous movement of Penitentism or *Hermanos
Penitentes*, which originated within the Catholic Church
but was later disavowed. Whether Catholic or of other
denominations, Mexican Americans usually attend separate churches. The Pomona study found that only two
out of every ten church-going adults went to Anglo
American churches.[17]

Of equal importance—although there are no specific
studies on this subject—is the distinctive nature of their
Catholicism; as in Latin America generally, it differs
significantly from Roman Catholicism in the United
States. Such conclusions as that of a recent study made
in Racine, Wisconsin, that the "religious ties" of the
Mexican Americans are "weak" [18] or of an earlier study
made in San Jose, California, that "most of them are
only nominal Catholics" [19] must be approached cau-
tiously. Further investigation would reveal, I think, that
what appear to be "weak ties" are actually *different* ties.
Those features which characterize Catholicism in this
country, so markedly stamped by the predominance of
an Irish "constituency," may be weak, but other distinctive features exist. For example, the sacrament of mar-
riage is often disregarded, but the sacrament of baptism
is closely adhered to by Mexican Americans. Various
authors have noted that Mexican American men are
less observant than women—it is quite usual for them
to cite the view (prevalent in many Latin countries

on both sides of the Atlantic) that "religion is for women." [20] Thus only a handful of men, other than the very old, may attend church regularly, and yet many of those who do not would be resentful if anyone were to disparage their Catholic faith.

Some observers have reported that the church continues to exercise a strong influence in the Mexican American community.[21] For example, Broom and Shevky contend that "the church is the principal agency of cultural conservatism for Mexicans in the United States and reinforces the separateness of the group." [22] They specify that they have in mind not only the parish organization of the Catholic Church but also the Protestant missions "with their functionally sectarian attributes." There seems to be little doubt that the "religious factor" (to use Professor Lenski's phrase) plays an important role in the rate of acculturation of Mexican Americans.

Cultural Characteristics and Acculturation

Although the limited assimilation and acculturation of Mexican Americans have often been commented on by social scientists, there are very few scholarly studies of the factors accounting for this situation. A recent effort along these lines is that of Florence Kluckhohn, who relates the slow rate of assimilation to sharp differences between the "deeply rooted" value orientations of the original Mexican culture and those of the dominant American culture. She shows that the two cultures have contrasting orientations toward some basic universal human problems. Thus the answer to the problem as to the relation of man to nature is "Subjugation-to-Nature" in the Mexican culture, but "Mastery-over-Nature" in the American culture. The note of fatalism in the attitudes and behavior of Mexican Americans springs from the orientation that the environment cannot be controlled. As for time orientation, the former stresses the present and the latter the future. Mexican Americans regard the future as both vague and unpredictable. Planning for the future, so characteristic of American culture, is therefore not their way of life.

The two cultures also have very different orientations toward the problem of desirable kinds of activity. The Mexican culture utilizes the alternative of "Being," that is, the preference for the kind of activity which is "a spontaneous expression of what is conceived to be 'given' in the personality." This preference finds expression in the elaborate pattern of fiesta activities. It is antithetical to the "Doing" orientation of the American culture, whose distinctive feature is "a demand for the kind of *activity* which results in accomplishments that are measurable by standards conceived to be external to the acting individual." [23] In the appraisal of persons, the primary questions in the American scale are, "What does the individual do? What can he or will he accomplish?" [24] but in the Mexican scale the primary questions are, *"quien es?"* (who is he?) and *"que classe de persona?"* (what kind of person?).

Kluckhohn also analyzes the contrasting definition of man's relation to other men as inherent in the two cultures. In the Mexican culture the "lineal" principle is dominant, that is, the continuity of the group through time is the crucial issue, and it is dealt with by a hierarchy of ordered positions. As we shall see later in more detail, this theme is reflected in the strong family and kinship ties of the Mexican Americans. This value orientation stands in sharp contrast to what Kluckhohn designates as the "individualistic principle" dominant in the American culture: individual goals have primacy over the goals of lineal groups such as the family.

The continuing strength of traditional cultural norms and the slow rate of assimilation of Mexican Americans, as Carolyn Zeleny has noted, are more characteristic of minorities in Europe than of other minorities in the United States. This is due in part to the fact that Mexican American history in this country began with the American conquest of territories in which they lived.[25] The twentieth century Mexican immigrants who came to the United States found here an indigenous Spanish-speaking population of long standing. They have not founded immigrant colonies so much as they have "moved in with their relatives." Contributing to cultural persistence and limited assimilation is the proximity to Mexico. Thus Carey McWilliams points out that, for the European immigrant to the United States, "the Atlantic crossing was of the utmost psychological and sociological importance; it was a severance, a crossing, an abrupt transition. But Mexican immigrants have seldom ventured beyond the fan of Spanish influence in the borderlands. . . ."[26]

Spatial Separateness

These various circumstances have helped to isolate Mexican Americans from the mainstream in the United States. Their position as casual laborers, connected with instability of employment and frequent migration, is also a factor in their institutional and spatial isolation.[27]

In southwestern towns and cities with any sizable Mexican American population there are residential ghettos of Mexican Americans. The residents refer to these enclaves as *colonia,* or *barrio* (neighborhood), but the dominant groups speak of them as "Little Mexico," "Mextown," or "Spiktown." About three fourths of all Mexican Americans in the United States live in the *colonias.*[28]

It is too often overlooked that from time to time there have been attempts on the part of Mexican Americans to break out of these ghettos, but these have been

largely unsuccessful and have met strong opposition by
the majority population. Paul S. Taylor, in his study of
the San Joaquin Valley in Southern California, shows
that as far back as the 1920s some Mexican Americans
tried, but were prevented from, moving out of the *colonia*. He emphasizes that "social pressure" was very
effective "in retarding movement out of the colony and
particularly of those who are rising just above the level
of the lowest group and who begin to feel the urge of
social ambition." [29]

These largely frustrated attempts to follow a generally legitimate and indeed highly valued pattern of mobility are part of the history of even those areas where
no "rigid" line of segregation exists today, for example,
San Antonio, Texas, and Los Angeles. Here, as else-
where, the Mexican American population continues
to be highly concentrated in separate neighborhoods.
These two communities deserve special comment since
they contain about one fourth of the entire Mexican
American population of the Southwest. San Antonio
is the city with the highest proportion of Mexican
Americans (40 percent of the total population), and
the population of Los Angeles includes more Mexican
Americans than that of any other city in this country.
It is estimated that over three fourths of all Mexican
Americans in San Antonio live in one section of the
city, the West Side;[30] in Los Angeles 75 percent of the
Mexican Americans live in 18 percent of the census
tracts.[31]

The most recent systematic study on this subject
found Mexican Americans to be highly segregated from
the majority population in most of the thirty-five cities
of the Southwest that it examined. However, in none
of these cities did the Mexican Americans approach the
degree of segregation of Negroes.[32] This conclusion was
based on the analysis of the 1960 Census tract data by
means of an index of segregation ranging from 0 to

100. (Zero would indicate no segregation and 100 would mean complete segregation.) The index of Mexican American segregation from Anglo Americans ranges from a low of 30 in Sacramento, California, to a high of 76 in Odessa, Texas, with a mean of 54. (The mean of Negro segregation from whites is 80 and the range from 57 to 94.) Further analysis by Moore and Mittlebach shows that a high index of Mexican American segregation from Anglo Americans is associated with a low proportion of foreign born and a low rate of population increase among them.[33]

When we speak of cities with no "rigid line" of segregation against Mexican Americans, we simply mean the relative absence of the type of segregation that applies to the Negro population. It by no means indicates that there is no discrimination against Mexican Americans, which does exist even in such cities as San Antonio and Los Angeles. The patterns of discrimination operating to maintain residential segregation are far from extinct. There are, however, some indications that they are on the decrease. The findings of the Pomona study confirm the notion prevalent in the Southwest that more of the younger and better educated Mexican American couples are moving out of the *colonia* and settling in new and better residential areas.[34] Yet it must be recognized that the residential separateness of Mexican Americans is also to a large extent the result of an economic situation: the financial inability to move out of the ghettos.

When turning our attention to the Mexican American youth of today, we shall see that they bear the marks of present and past segregation and social isolation.

Notes

1. U. S. Bureau of Census, *1960 Census of Population, Persons of Spanish Surname*, Final Report PC(2)-1B, Washington, D. C., 1963, Table 1; *Characteristics of the Population*, Vol. 1, Part 1, Washington, D. C., 1961, Table 10; State Volumes, Tables 13 and 15.

2. Carey McWilliams, *North from Mexico—The Spanish-Speaking People of the United States*, Philadelphia: Lippincott, 1949, p. 7.

3. Clark S. Knowlton, "The Spanish Americans in New Mexico," *Sociology and Social Research*, 45 (July, 1961), pp. 448-55.

4. Bogue, *op. cit.*, p. 352; Constantine Panuncio, *How Mexicans Earn and Live*, Berkeley: University of California Press, 1933, p. 2.

5. Lyle Saunders, *Cultural Differences and Medical Care: The Case of Spanish Speaking People in the Southwest*, New York: Russell Sage Foundation, 1954, pp. 300-7.

6. Hutchinson, *op. cit.*, p. 59.

7. Manuel Gamio, *Mexican Immigration to the United States—A Study of Human Migration and Adjustment*, Chicago: University of Chicago Press, 1930, p. 54.

8. U. S. Bureau of Census, *Persons of Spanish Surname, op. cit.*, Tables 1, 5, and 6; U. S. Bureau of Census, *1960 Census of Population, Characteristics of the Population, op. cit.*, Tables 96 and 97; State Volumes, Table 57.

9. *Background for Planning*, Los Angeles: Research Department, Welfare Planning Council, 1963, p. xxxiii.

10. *Persons of Spanish Surname, op. cit.*, Tables 3 and 7; U. S. Bureau of Census, *1960 Census of Population, Educational Attainment*, Washington, D. C., 1961, Tables 1 and 2; *Characteristics of the Population, op. cit.*, Table 174; State Volumes, Table 47.

11. Broom and Shevky, *op. cit.*, p. 154.

12. Fernando Penalosa, "Class Consciousness and Social Mobility in a Mexican-American Community." Unpublished Ph.D. dissertation, University of Southern California, 1963. Pp. 99, 327.

13. Tuck, *op. cit.*, p. 133; Margaret Clark, *Health in the Mexican-American Culture*, Berkeley: University of California Press, 1959, pp. 16-19; Ossie G. Simmons, "Anglo-Americans

and Mexican-Americans in South Texas." Unpublished Ph.D. dissertation, Harvard University, 1952. P. 339.

14. George C. Barker, "Social Functions of Language in a Mexican-American Community," *Acta Americana*, 4 (July-September, 1947), pp. 189-92.

15. Penalosa, *op. cit.*, pp. 289-93, 324.

16. Clark, *op. cit.*, p. 22.

17. Penalosa, *op. cit.*, p. 147.

18. This was a study of in-migration in Racine, Wisconsin. Its aim was to examine factors which facilitate or impede the assimilation of immigrants to the area, especially Mexican Americans and Negroes. See: Lyle W. Shannon and Elaine M. Krass, *The Economic Absorption and Cultural Integration of Inmigrant Mexican-American and Negro Workers*, Iowa City: State University of Iowa, Department of Sociology and Anthropology, 1964, p. 197.

19. Clark, *op. cit.*, p. 110.

20. Beatrice Griffith, *American Me*, Boston: Houghton Mifflin, 1948, p. 184; Clark, *op. cit.*, p. 133.

21. Penalosa, *op. cit.*, p. 141; Broom and Shevky, *op. cit.*, p. 157.

22. Broom and Shevky, *ibid.*

23. Florence R. Kluckhohn and Fred Strodtbeck, *Variations in Value Orientations*, New York: Row, Peterson, 1961, pp. 1-49, 175-257.

24. *Ibid.*, p. 18.

25. Related in McWilliams, *op. cit.*, p. 207.

26. *Ibid.*, p. 58.

27. Broom and Shevky, *op. cit.*, p. 153.

28. John H. Burma, *Spanish-Speaking Groups in the United States*, Durham: Duke University Press, 1954, p. 88.

29. Paul S. Taylor, *Mexican Labor in the United States— Migration Statistics*, Berkeley: University of California Press, 1929, p. 82. See also: McWilliams, *op. cit.*, pp. 187-9.

30. Jack E. Dodson, "Minority Group Housing in Two Texas Cities," in Nathan Glazer and Davis McEntire, eds., *Studies in Housing and Minority Groups*, Berkeley: University of California Press, 1960, p. 93.

31. Celia Stopnicka Heller, "Ambitions of Mexican-American Youth—Goals and Means of Mobility of High School Seniors." Unpublished Ph.D. dissertation, Columbia University, 1963. Pp. 22-3.

32. *Progress Report*, No. 1, Mexican-American Study Project, Graduate School of Business Administration, University of California, Los Angeles, January 3, 1965, p. 3.

33. It is the same index as the index of dissimilarity used by Duncan and other urban analysts. For details, see: Joan W. Moore and Frank G. Mittlebach, "Residential Segregation of Minorities in the Urban Southwest," paper presented at the annual meeting of the American Sociological Association, Chicago, Illinois, 1965.

34. Penalosa, *op. cit.*, p. 163.

THREE

The Youth of Today

The main theme running through the following chapters is pointed up by the question: to what extent is the Mexican American youth of today bound by, and to what extent does he transcend, the kind of background sketched in the preceding chapters? We shall begin with the principal general characteristics of Mexican American younger people and end with a discussion of some of the major obstacles they face.

Size of the Youth Population

One of the striking features of the Mexican American group is that its population is young. (See Figure 1.) Its median age is close to 20, as compared with about 30 years for the total U. S. white population.

Noteworthy is the large contrast between those who were born in Mexico, with a median age of 43, and the native born, with a median age of 16 years.

Teenagers constitute about 21 percent of the Mexican American, and 16 percent of the Anglo American, population in the Southwest. Of the 717,740 Mexican Americans who are between 10 and 19 years old, over half, 360,760, are male. If "youth" is defined as the ages 15 to 19, then one may speak of the Mexican

Figure 1   AGE DISTRIBUTION OF TWO POPULATION GROUPS IN FIVE SOUTHWESTERN STATES,* BY SEX: 1960**

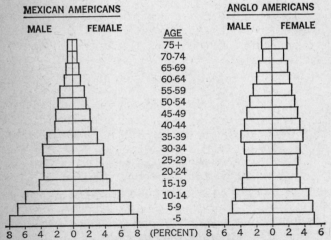

*Includes ARIZONA, CALIFORNIA, COLORADO, NEW MEXICO, AND TEXAS.
**From the files of the Mexican-American Study Project,
    University of California, Los Angeles.

American youth as around 300,000 in number. Of these, about half (over 153,000) are males.[1]

Distinguishing Characteristics

In physical appearance Mexican American youth are far from homogeneous. As George Sanchez describes them, "Biologically, they range over all the possible combinations of, first, their heterogeneous Spanish antecedents and, then, the *mestizaje* resulting from the crossing of Spaniards and various indigenous peoples of Mexico. . . ." [2] To this, one could add that insofar as they are predominantly American born, they are also apt to show some physiological effects of the American environment. An anthropological investigation has discovered that, similar to the children of other immigrant groups in the United States,* the American-born sons of Mexican-born fathers display such physical changes as increase in stature, hand length, and decrease in nasal index.[3]

The *differentia specifica* between the Mexican American and the Anglo American youth is not United States birth but rather non-Mexican origin. Because of common misconceptions, it should be stressed that nine out of ten Mexican American youths (ages 15 to 19) are native born, and that both parents of six out of ten were born in the United States. Thus the majority are at least third-generation American.[4]

Whether they are first, second, or third generation, their principal language, especially in interpersonal relationships, seems to be a form of American Spanish, that is, a local Spanish dialect heavily intermingled with his-

---

* In 1912 Franz Boas first demonstrated that American-born descendants of immigrants undergo bodily changes, but the cause of such changes, apart from the increase in stature, is as yet unknown. (See: Ashley Montagu, *Human Heredity*, New York: Mentor Books, 1960, pp. 101-2.)

panized English terms and anglicized Spanish words. The Texas Spanish, for example, is known as "Tex-Mex." [5] A highly specialized dialect is *Pachuco*, but since it is mainly the language of delinquent youths, we shall describe it in Chapter Five, which focuses upon this subject.

Many of the children were first introduced to English in school. That the schools largely fail in their minimal function of teaching the native tongue to Mexican Americans is reflected in the language difficulties with which these youths are plagued. Although no systematic studies of their language pattern have been conducted in recent years,* various writers have emphasized their language handicap and have noted that a foreign accent in English is common among second- and third-generation Mexican American youths.[6] This is a cause of considerable embarrassment and often results in their feeling self-conscious when in contact with Anglo Americans. Frequently Mexican American youths are deficient in informal English: they do not know how to "kid" or use "small talk," so important in everyday encounters. Still, they do not, as a rule, seem to encourage the rare efforts of Anglo Americans to speak Spanish to them, but tend to respond in English. It is likely that they perceive such attempts as a way of "talking down" to them. Also, they seem embarrassed by their "poor Spanish."

The language problem of the Mexican Americans, however, is not insurmountable. Both common sense

---

* The latest work is that of George C. Barker, "Social Functions of Language in a Mexican-American Community," *op. cit.*, pp. 185-202. The recent Racine and Pomona studies do report on the language of Mexican Americans but they are based on the questioning of adults about their own and their children's language rather than on observation. Furthermore, the language of the children in Racine and Pomona may lean more toward English as compared with the children of the Southwest in general. (See: Shannon and Krass, *op. cit.*, p. 299; Penalosa, *op. cit.*, pp. 104-20.)

and available research[7] indicate that language does not necessarily have to be a permanent intellectual handicap for children born into foreign-language-speaking homes. Furthermore, any programs geared to overcoming the English language difficulties of Mexican American children would have in their favor the factor of Mexican heritage of verbal articulateness. Verbal mastery is a highly cherished value among Latin American males of all classes and finds reflection in the fluency of language and extensiveness of vocabulary even among those of humble origin and position.[8]

One of the few programs is the campaign started by LULAC, a Mexican American voluntary organization (League of United Latin American Citizens), to teach children going into elementary school four hundred basic English words. The campaign was subsequently taken up by the state authorities in Texas.[9] But apart from such programs, distinct changes are coming to the forefront. These should be noted especially because the preservation of the Spanish language by Mexican Americans has been interpreted as "a persistent symbol and instrument of isolation." [10] It has been observed that from the Anglo point of view the wide use of Spanish is the primary symbol of the "foreignness" of the Mexican Americans, but from the latters' viewpoint it is the primary symbol of loyalty to *La Raza*.[11] And yet one notices the beginning of a new pattern of language behavior among Mexican Americans today which manifested itself among other immigrant groups in the second generation. Parents speak American Spanish to their children and the children respond in English. In Pomona, for example, 65 percent of the interviewed Mexican Americans who had children reported that their children spoke only English to them.[12] (Of course, one must keep in mind that the Mexican Americans of Pomona are more acculturated than those in many other parts of the Southwest.) Then, too, there is a growing awareness among Mexican Americans that language skills are necessary for socioeconomic advancement.[13] An increasing number of parents are forcing themselves to speak English at home so as to "make it easier" for their children. For instance, Margaret Clark quotes a Mexican American woman: "Since my husband and I knew that our children would probably have teachers who don't know our language, we were always careful to speak some English around the house so that the children would have an easier time in school." [14]

Family Size and Its Implications

To this day probably most Mexican American parents continue to be unaware of the extent to which each child's chances for advancement are hampered by the large number of siblings. There is little room for dispute that, in general, the size of a family is inversely related to its upward mobility.[15] My recent study of Mexican American high school seniors supports the contention that Mexican Americans are no exception to this general relationship—students with fewer siblings had more means for realizing their occupational aspirations than others. Moreover, there was as much as ten points of difference in the average I. Q. scores of Mexican American boys with only one sibling or none and those who had four or more siblings. As many as 43 percent of the former but only 14 percent of the latter pursued an academic course of study. Furthermore, three times as many boys with up to three siblings anticipated finishing college or pursuing graduate studies as those with four or more siblings.

This study suggests the idea that an important factor in the slow upward mobility of Mexican Americans, which has not been sufficiently explored, is their high birth rate. The importance of family size in this respect is supported by the finding that, while the avenues of mobility of Mexican American students differed significantly with size of family, they did not differ much with parental occupation, education, or country of birth.[16]

Table 2 PERCENTAGE DISTRIBUTION OF FAMILIES WITH OWN CHILDREN UNDER EIGHTEEN YEARS OF AGE, BY NUMBER OF CHILDREN: 1960

Number of Children	"White" Families in the United States	Mexican American Families* in the Five Southwestern States
1	32.8	23.6
2	32.5	24.2
3	19.2	19.4
4 or more children	15.5	32.9
TOTAL	100.0%	100.1%

SOURCES: U. S. Census of Population: 1960, *Families*, Final Report PC(2)-4A, Table 5; U. S. Census of Population: 1960, *Persons of Spanish Surname*, Final Report PC(2)-1B, Table 5.

* Mexican American stands for families with Spanish surname.

A glance at Table 2 shows clearly that Mexican American youths as a whole come from much larger families than those of the "white" segment of the population. The proportion of families with four or more children (of the total families with children under 18) is twice as high among Mexican Americans as among "whites" in general. Such large families constitute one third of all Mexican American families with children under 18. Although there are no known studies specifically devoted to this subject, some evidence exists that the family among Mexican Americans has not become smaller in size than has the family in Mexico, nor does it vary in size with generations in the United States.[17]

Home Socialization

Not only in size, but also in organization, the Mexican American family displays an unusual persistence of traditional forms. It continues to be an extended type of family with strong ties spread through a number of generations in a large web of kinship. These ties impose obligations of mutual aid, respect, and affection. The kinship ties are extended even beyond genetic links by the institution known as *compadrazgo*. The *compadres*, not blood relatives, assume what are in fact family obligations in a religious ceremony establishing ritual kinship. For example, parents and godparents are *compadres* and have a right to seek help and advice from each other.

In its authority structure, the family is also highly traditional. Family authority within the nuclear unit is vested in the father or, in case of his absence, in the oldest male wage earner.[18] According to the traditional norms, the husband is regarded as the authoritarian, patriarchal figure who is both the head and the master of the family and the mother as the affectional figure in the family. In the words of Oscar Lewis, "His prerogatives are to receive the obedience and respect of his wife and children, as well as their services." Actually, the wife exercises a considerable amount of control within the home, especially concerning the children, since "husbands keep aloof from the petty details of the household." [19] In the Mexican American home the division of labor between the sexes is sharply defined, resting on a sexually based dichotomous set of cultural expectations: throughout life males are accorded higher status than females.[20]

The kind of socialization that Mexican American children generally receive at home is not conducive to the development of the capacities needed for advancement in a dynamic industrialized society. This type of upbringing creates stumbling blocks to future advancement by stressing values that hinder mobility—family ties, honor, masculinity, and living in the present—and by neglecting the values that are conducive to it—achievement, independence, and deferred gratification.

Of particular importance in forging family ties is the sense of responsibility that the child acquires toward his younger siblings. From the age of five or six, a child may be responsible for his younger brother or sister. With this responsibility also comes a growing authority of older over younger, approximating parental control.[21] Younger children are usually as much in awe of an older brother as they are of their parents.

This early training finds full expression in the adolescent boy's assumption of the role of guardian and protector of his sisters, both younger and older, and of his younger brothers. The role of the brother—similar to the situation in Mexico itself—begins, in a sense, as the extension of the father's role. In Mexico the father's position is invested with great authority over his wife and children, and some of his power is extended to the "grown sons." But in the Mexican American family in the United States the "grown boy's" role, which begins in adolescence, and particularly that of the oldest son, has a quality distinct from that of the father's role. He is the link with the outside world and acts as mentor in the American outlook and American practices for his younger siblings. Thus he "becomes protector, orderer, and forbidder, in short a foster parent schooled in American ways."[22] In acting out this role, the Mexican American boy may even commit acts which bring him to the attention of the police.

This role is colored by the image of the ideal male personality which is held up before the male child, irrespective of the social position of the family. This image includes sexual prowess, physical strength, adventurousness and courage, male dominance, self-confidence, and verbal articulation.[23] Ruth Tuck notes that "Boys and girls are given a differential upbringing. The girl is trained for the home, the boy for the world." [24] This differential socialization is consistent with their future adult roles. The norm is that the husband, being a male, cannot be expected to remain faithful to his wife, but the wife owes the husband absolute sexual fidelity and is expected to regard the peccadillos of her husband with tolerance. Male children are indulged, and boys are given a good deal of freedom of movement for which they are not expected to account to their parents. Their outside activities are considered part of the process of becoming a man. Such indulgent attitudes of parents have been shown by David McClelland and others to hamper in their sons the development of the "need of achievement" in educational and occupational endeavors.[25]

On the other hand, girls are closely supervised and taught that their place is in the home,[26] although there is some indication that the norms of feminine behavior may be changing in the direction of more freedom.[27] However, this seems to be not so much a result of changes in early home socialization as a product of the adolescent girl's revolt against female confinement at home.

The theme of honor, like that of *machismo* (manliness), is predominant in the orientation the Mexican American child receives at home. Honor in this conception is tied to an inner integrity which every child inherits as part of his Mexican American birthright and which he is to guard jealously against all. It manifests itself in "extreme sensitivity to insult" [28] displayed so often by Mexican American youths. Their reactions, consistent with their concept of honor, seen from the Anglo American standpoint, often appear as "touchiness."

Tied to the values of honor and respect is the emphasis which the home places on respectful conduct. It is a sign of *persona educada* and is stressed as behavior to be learned by all, irrespective of social class. The individual who lacks it is *bruto* or *burro,* an out-model of which the child is often reminded. Both boys and girls are urged to show respect, obedience, and humility in their behavior toward parents and elders and are drilled in courtesy.[29] In many homes, for example, the child is taught to respond to the parents' or elders' call of his name with the phrase *mande usted,* at your command. As Ruth Tuck observes, "Good manners stand high in the list of desirable attributes for children, even in humble homes." [30] This value is reflected in the everyday behavior of Mexican American youth, which is marked by extraordinary courtesy and politeness as compared, at least on the basis of casual observation, with that of Anglo American youth of the same socio-economic status. It should be noted that Mexican American youths do not think of this kind of behavior as "good manners" but rather as "being respectful." When questioned whether their home stresses good manners they tended to answer in the negative and point to school as the place where they are stressed. Yet the same boys related at length how they were taught at home to be respectful and how they try and do conform to this rule.

But honor and politeness are not strategic values for young people in the development of mobility aspirations, which require a more direct orientation toward the goal of occupational success. Mexican American children do not receive this kind of training at home. Parents, as a whole, neither impose standards of excellence for tasks performed by their children nor do they communicate to them that they expect evidence of high achievement. The parents' great love for their children is not conditional: it does not depend on the child's level of performance as compared with his peers—a widely reported trait among middle class Anglo American parents.[31] Although conditional love is not the only known mechanism for early socialization in achievement, other mechanisms with that function, comparable, for example, to that of "shame" among Jews and Japanese, are also lacking. Unlike some children in these minority groups, the Mexican American child is not prodded to achieve or risk bringing shame on himself and his family.

This lack of emphasis upon "making good" in conventional terms is consistent with the themes of fatalism and resignation which run through Mexican American culture. What it lacks is the idea, so characteristic of modal American culture, that the individual can command the future to serve his own ends. The contrast between the former's present-time orientation and the latter's future-time orientation is striking, borne out in the conspicuous fact that the Mexican American home does not cultivate in the children the ability to defer gratification which, according to many contemporary studies, is conducive to upward mobility.[32]

The combination of stress on work and rational use of time to which Anglo American children, especially in families sharing middle class values, are exposed at home forms little or no part of the Mexican American socialization process.[33] Time tends to be disregarded when it interferes with other values, such as rest, thought, and enjoyment. Mexican Americans have retained the conception of work as, at best, a necessary concession: the child learns at home that work, although the common lot of the people around him, is a necessity, not a virtue. Also stressed in his home environment is the notion that inactivity and leisure are dignified and worthwhile goals, and these values are reinforced by the inculcation of supportive attitudes. There is the consequent learning of "lax" habits and the failure to develop habits of self-discipline and time manipulation.

The home also fails to provide the kind of independence training that, as brought out in various investigations, is highly functional for achievement.[34] This is the sort of training in which parents communicate to the child that they expect him to be self-reliant and grant him relative autonomy in decision making situations. In contrast to this orientation, as Florence Kluckhohn notes, Mexican American children are "vigorously trained for dependent behavior as the average Anglo-American child is schooled for independence." It is not surprising, therefore, that these children seldom show initiative or freely express their own ideas.[35]

Finally, few Mexican American homes stress higher education or intellectual effort. That parental influence and pressure to go to college are an important determinant of whether a working class boy will obtain a higher education has been convincingly demonstrated by Joseph Kahl in his article on "'Common Men' Boys."[36] And this mode of parental behavior is largely absent in the homes of Mexican American youth. Mexican American boys have often complained to me that they lacked encouragement from their parents, especially their fathers, to continue their schooling. This may be in part an indirect product of tension and conflict between father and son over authority. As we have seen, the authority of the son in the American setting is no longer simply an extension of the father's authority but rests on his being the mediator between the Mexican and American cultures. The father-son relationship seems to be profoundly disturbed in many of the Mexican American homes as the sons assume positions of dominance or of equality with their fathers.

The lack of parental encouragement to pursue a formal education may also be directly tied to the parents' belief that higher education is useless for their children and would not result in achievement but rather lead to frustration and humiliation. To help their children avoid this situation, some parents cite those Mexican Americans who have received a college education but who have nevertheless failed to move into occupations for which they are technically qualified.[37] One young Mexican American, for example, told me: "My father always says: 'you don't need to go to school. You will have to work anyway.'"

The questionnaire responses of the recent Racine study seem to be consistent with the above observations based on qualitative data. Mexican American as well as Anglo American and Negro parents were asked how much schooling they would "like" their children to have. Only 25 percent of the Mexican Americans, in contrast to 50 percent of the Negroes and 67 percent of the Anglo Americans, mentioned college. When questioned whether they would be satisfied with various levels of education actually reached by their children, more Mexican Americans said that they would be content with a minimal amount than did either the Anglo Americans or the Negroes (37 percent of the Mexican Americans but only 6 percent of the Anglo Americans thought that they would be satisfied if their children received only a junior high school education). And finally, a substantially higher percentage of Mexican Americans than either Anglo Americans or Negroes felt that it would be "practically impossible," considering their financial condition, to keep their children in school beyond the ninth grade.[38]

To be sure, a change is beginning to take place in the attitudes toward education among Mexican Americans. Some parents are now encouraging their sons to continue their schooling. I recall, for instance, a young student who, during my interview with him, gave this reply to my question as to what prompted his decision to go to college:

I guess I've always wanted to go to college. There was much value placed on education at home. . . . My father, in his uneducated way, was always reading to us kids, and I remember a game he used to play with the dictionary, in which he would read words and let us guess their meanings. He would then give us the dictionary and let us quiz him. As he would rattle off how much he knew, I can still remember the look on his face of great proudness of what he had learned.

But such parents are still the exception among Mexican Americans.[39] Generally, their children experience a kind of socialization that, on the one hand, reinforces traditional values and, on the other, is dysfunctional for achievement in conventional terms. Thus, in examining the Mexican American youth of today—both the ambitious and the delinquent, as well as the majority who fall between these polar types—we should keep in mind the fact that they have first entered school having already acquired a relative inability for and disinterest in the success tasks that are commonly set in school.

Notes

1. The figures are from the 1960 Census and the percentages were calculated on the basis of these figures. See: *Persons of Spanish Surname, op. cit.,* Table 2; the figures on the total white population are from: *Characteristics of the Population, op. cit.,* Table 65; for the Southwest, from: State volumes, Table 17.

2. Quoted in McWilliams, *op. cit.,* p. 42.

3. Marcus S. Goldstein, *Demographic and Bodily Changes in Descendants of Mexican Immigrants,* Austin: University of Texas, Institute of Latin-American Studies, 1943; M. F. Ashley Montagu, *An Introduction to Physical Anthropology,* Springfield: Charles C Thomas, 1951, p. 423.

4. Calculations based on 1960 Census figures which appear in: *Persons of Spanish Surname, op. cit.,* Table 2.

5. Sherif, *op. cit.,* Table 2.

6. Simmons, *op. cit.,* pp. 407, 419-20; Richard G. Thurston, "Urbanization and Socio-cultural Change in a Mexican-American

Enclave." Unpublished Ph.D. dissertation, University of California, Los Angeles, 1957. P. 205; Broom and Shevky, *op. cit.*, p. 153; Clark, *op. cit.*, pp. 24-25.

7. Leona E. Tyler, *The Psychology of Human Differences*, New York: Appleton, 1956, p. 305.

8. John Gillin, "Ethos Components in Modern Latin-American Culture," *American Anthropologist*, 57 (June, 1955), p. 497; Oscar Lewis, *The Children of Sanchez*, New York: Random House, 1961, p. xxii.

9. Jane MacWab Christian and Chester Christian, Jr., "Spanish Language and Culture in the Southwest," in Joshua A. Fishman, ed., "Language Loyalty in the United States," A Final Report to the U. S. Office of Education, Language Research Section, Vol. 3, p. 38.

10. Broom and Shevky, *op. cit.*, p. 153.

11. William Madsen, *Mexican-Americans of South Texas*, New York: Holt, Rinehart and Winston, 1964, p. 106.

12. Penalosa, *op. cit.*, p. 120.

13. Arthur J. Rubel, "Social Life of Urban Mexican Americans." Unpublished Ph.D. dissertation, University of North Carolina, 1962. P. 49.

14. Clark, *op. cit.*, p. 55.

15. S. M. Lipset and R. Bendix, *Social Mobility in Industrial Society*, Berkeley: University of California Press, 1962, pp. 240-1.

16. Heller, *op. cit.*, pp. 114-15, 141, 164-7. For an analysis of the data about Anglo American high school seniors in Los Angeles, see: Ralph Turner, *The Social Context of Ambition*, San Francisco: Chandler, 1965. The data about Mexican Americans, which he collected but did not utilize, he generously made available to me.

17. Thurston, *op. cit.*, pp. 51, 211.

18. Robert C. Jones, "Ethnic Family Patterns: The Mexican Family in the United States," *American Journal of Sociology*, 53 (May, 1948), p. 450.

19. Oscar Lewis, "Husbands and Wives in a Mexican Village: A Study of Role Conflicts," in Olen E. Leonard and Charles P. Loomis, eds., *Readings in Latin American Social Organization and Institutions*, East Lansing: Michigan State College Press, 1953, pp. 23, 29.

20. Munro Edmonson, *Los Manitos—A Study of Institutional Values*, New Orleans: Middle American Research Institute, Tulane University, 1957, p. 32; R. Fernandez Marina, E. D. Maldonado-Sierra, and R. D. Trent, "Three Basic Themes in

Mexican and Puerto Rican Family Values," *Journal of Social Psychology*, 48 (November, 1958), pp. 167-81.

21. Ralph L. Beals, "Culture Patterns of Mexican-American Life," *Proceedings of the Fifth Annual Conference, Southwestern Council on Education of Spanish Speaking People*, Pepperdine College: January, 1951, p. 11; Kluckhohn and Strodtbeck, *op. cit.*, p. 197.

22. Norman D. Humphrey, "The Changing Structure of the Detroit Mexican Family: An Index of Acculturation," *American Sociological Review*, 9 (December, 1944), p. 625.

23. Simmons, *op. cit.*, p. 75; Arthur J. Rubel, "Concepts of Disease in Mexican-American Culture," *American Anthropologist* (October, 1960), pp. 810-14.

24. Tuck, *op. cit.*, p. 124.

25. See: David C. McClelland, *The Achieving Society*, Princeton: Van Nostrand, 1961, p. 356.

26. John H. Burma, *op. cit.*, p. 11.

27. Rubel, "Social Life of Urban Mexican Americans," *op. cit.*, p. 213.

28. Simmons, *op. cit.*, p. 115.

29. Rogelio Diaz Guerrero, "Neurosis and the Mexican Family Structure," *American Journal of Psychiatry*, 112 (December, 1955), p. 414.

30. Tuck, *op. cit.*, p. 124.

31. Kluckhohn and Strodtbeck, *op. cit.*, p. 197.

32. See, e.g.: Louis Schneider and Svere Lysgaard, "The Deferred Gratification Pattern: A Preliminary Study," *American Sociological Review*, 22 (February, 1957), pp. 67-73.

33. Burma, *op. cit.*, p. 9.

34. See, e.g.: Bernard C. Rosen, "Race, Ethnicity, and the Achievement Syndrome," *American Sociological Review*, 22 (February, 1959), pp. 48-60; Bernard C. Rosen, "Socialization and Achievement Motivation in Brazil," *American Sociological Review*, 27 (October, 1962), pp. 612-25; D. C. McClelland, A. Rindlisbacher, and R. de Charms, "Religious and Other Sources of Parental Attitude Toward Independence Training," in D. C. McClelland, ed., *Studies in Motivation*, New York: Appleton, 1955, pp. 389-97.

35. Kluckhohn and Strodtbeck, *op. cit.*, p. 197.

36. Joseph A. Kahl, "Educational and Occupational Aspirations of 'Common Men' Boys," *Harvard Educational Review*, 23 (1953), pp. 186-203.

37. Tuck, *op. cit.*, pp. 189-90; Kluckhohn and Strodtbeck, *op. cit.*, p. 248.

38. Shannon and Krass, *op. cit.*, pp. 240-4.

39. Claire L. Peterson, "When the Migrant Laborer Settles Down—A Report of the Findings of a Project on Value Assimilation of Immigrant Laborers," mimeographed, University of Wisconsin, 1964, p. 25.

FOUR

The School Experience

Our public school philosophy is based on the assumption that education is not the sole responsibility of parents but that at a certain point society, or rather its agencies, must step in and take over the task of educating its members. This being the case, it is important to examine to what extent schools realize this aim, especially with such groups of children as the Mexican Americans whose homes do not prepare them for adequate functioning in our society.

Many Mexican American parents recognize their inability and failure to develop in their children the facility to deal with the non-Mexican environment. However, they do not seem aware of the fact that the schools, too, fail the Mexican American children in this respect. These conclusions, based on conversations with parents, are supported by the findings of the Racine study. When asked: "where do children learn more—in school, in the home, or when they go to work," 22 percent of the Mexican Americans, but 62 percent of the Anglo Americans, mentioned home, or home and other factors. As many as 74 percent of the Mexican Americans, compared with 29 percent of the Anglo Americans, named the schools only.[1]

Scholastic Performance

As has been shown, Mexican American children enter school without the kind of experience on which school life is based. Under the circumstances, it would not be surprising if their scholastic performance were poorer than that of Anglo American children at the start of their schooling. Yet, several studies have shown that Mexican American children tend to start out on much the same level as the Anglo American children, both in I. Q. scores and scholastic achievement. It may, however, seem tragic that the longer Mexican Americans stay in school, the less they resemble the other children in these endeavors.[2] One of the most recent investigations, that of Los Angeles high school seniors, dramatically reinforces these findings. Here is a group of Mexican American students, products of public schools, who were so highly motivated to continue their education as to resist the prevalent tendency to drop out of school before their senior year. After 11 years of schooling, their I. Q. distribution did not correspond to the "normal I. Q. curve." Almost half of them, in contrast to 13 percent of the Anglo Americans, were below average in I. Q. Only six percent of the Mexican Americans but 28 percent of the Anglo American high school seniors scored above average.[3]

What are the schools like which these Mexican American children have been attending? Until the late forties, Mexican American children were *formally* segregated in separate buildings or separate schools. The rationalization was that these children knew little or no English on entering school, could not compete on an equal basis with Anglo American children, and it was therefore best for both groups to be separated. In California, in 1947, the courts decided, in the *Mendez* case, that enforced segregation violated the United States Constitution. A similar decision, in the *Delgado* case, was rendered in Texas in 1948.[4] Today, the schools attended by Mexican Americans are located in the poorest areas and thus are largely segregated on a *de facto* basis.

These schools generally do not make the first exposure to American values and skills the exciting experience it could be. As a rule, no designs have been worked out and incorporated into educational programs to enhance the early experiences in school or to facilitate the transition from the Mexican home to the American school. According to a recent study, most teachers were found to believe that the same type of curriculum could essentially satisfy the needs of both Mexican American and Anglo American children.[5] As George Sanchez put it 25 years ago—and it still seems to apply today—the school program generally proceeds on the "fallacious assumption" that all children come from homes with American cultural standards and traditions.[6]

Teacher-Student Relations

The blame for the poor scholastic record of Mexican American children has often been placed on the teachers. It appears in almost all the writings about Mexican Americans which touch on the problem of their low educational achievements. The "explanations" range from the general claim that teachers simply do not understand the Mexican American children to the specific charge that the teachers are hostile toward them.[7] The latter is illustrated by the following statement made by Carey McWilliams:

> Notoriously bad linguists, Anglo-American teachers have been known to show an unreasoning irritation over the mere sound of a Spanish word or phrase. . . . This irritation is often reflected in a hostile attitude toward Spanish-speaking students. Over a period of many years, I have heard Anglo-American teachers in the Southwest complain bitterly about the "stubbornness" of Mexican-American youngsters who will persist in speaking Spanish. . . .[8]

Even if one were to dismiss this as based on single experiences rather than rigorous evidence, the former observation that teachers generally fail to understand Mexican American children is supported by a number of studies. For example, Richard Thurston noted that none of the teachers in the community he investigated ever visited the neighborhood where their Mexican American pupils lived.[9] Again, a more recent study by Horacio Ulibarri found teachers to show little awareness of sociocultural factors affecting the classroom behavior of Mexican American children. These teachers were quite sensitive to the obvious fact of the pupils' English language deficiency but largely unaware of such basic issues as the meaningfulness, or lack of it, of the classroom experience for Mexican American children.[10]

Teachers today still tend to regard assignment to a school in a Mexican American district as an inferior one, bordering on punishment (as do teachers who are assigned to schools in areas heavily populated by Negroes). Their numerous complaints about the difficulties of teaching Mexican American children become more understandable in view of their ignorance of the children's background. For example, a teacher who, perhaps unknowingly, offends the Mexican American boy's sense of honor may find it very difficult to control him. As one perceptive Anglo American high school teacher noted, it was much easier for her to gain the cooperation of Mexican American boys by using, in her words, "extra-polite" language.

Lack of such knowledge and understanding may not only make it hard for teachers to instruct Mexican American children, but also to proceed in a way that would make it easier for the children to identify with their teachers. One college student, during an interview, had this comment about his fellow Mexican Americans during his high school days: "They don't take the teachers seriously. To them, when the teacher talks, she talks from the other side of the fence." Mexican American boys seem rarely to identify with their teachers. Thurston relates that, in the community he studied, "Reports of school experiences by Pueblo children . . . were predominantly negative or neutral. There did not appear to be much idealization of teachers." [11]

This situation merits further systematic study, since the teacher probably occupies a strategic position for influencing Mexican American upward mobility. One gains insight into the potential importance of this position when talking with Mexican Americans who have been occupationally successful. Careful questioning reveals that there is almost always an individual, often a teacher or principal, whom such mobile persons credit for their accomplishments. For example, a Mexican American college graduate described his school history: "I was discouraged about even going to elementary school until I reached the fifth grade. . . . I had been kicked out of four schools already as a problem child. In the fifth grade, at the California Street School, the principal, without asking any questions as to why I had transferred, asked whether I wanted to be a Safety Monitor. . . . From then on I became interested in school in spite of the fact that I was afraid the other boys would razz me for being a school stooge." [12] Another Mexican American, a student at the University of California, testified: "As long as I live I will never forget a sixth grade teacher I had. . . . Her encouragement made me want to make something of myself. She planted the seeds of college in my head. . . . Words of encouragement and acceptance meant a great deal to me." [13]

In this connection, Florence Kluckhohn, in her study of a Mexican American community, Atrisco, also points to the potential influence of the teacher on the acculturation of Mexican Americans. She describes one sympathetic teacher who was sought out by young and old alike for advice and support, and concludes that, had the community had more such teachers, "it is probable that a degree of familiarity with the Anglo dominated outside world would have been gained and gained without resentment." Not only were there no other teachers with her understanding and insight, but "even she was hampered in what she could do by a formal educational program which was not designed to meet the adjustive needs of Spanish-Americans." [14]

School Curricula

School guidance personnel, in addition to teachers, have been subjected to considerable criticism by individuals interested in the educational problems of Mexican American youth. The charge is often made against them that they deliberately guide Mexican American students into nonacademic subjects and thus limit their possibilities of reaching college.[15] The fact is that a much smaller proportion of Mexican American than of Anglo American high school students pursue an academic course of study. Thus, Ralph Turner's data on Los Angeles high school students show that one fifth of the Mexican Americans, as compared with one half of the Anglo Americans, followed an academic curriculum. But both school guidance personnel and teachers usually believe that they are merely being objective, citing the low I. Q. scores of Mexican American youth, in advising and encouraging them to pursue "practical" rather than academic programs. They do not see these scores for what they really are: products of peculiar social and cultural circumstances and indeed indicators of deficiency in schooling itself.[16]

Perhaps as often as being pushed by school personnel into industrial and vocational courses, Mexican American children simply drift into them. As one youth, who managed to finish college despite having followed an industrial high school course, explained: "Taking the industrial course was the easiest thing to do. It was the line of least resistance." [17] The "line of least resistance" may be a common pattern for the other Mexican American students who are handicapped in some of the things that go into achieving an adequate I. Q. score.

Dropouts

Another common pattern is to stop attending school as soon as possible. Thus the proportion of Mexican American youths, between 16 and 19 years old, who do not attend school is considerably higher than that of Anglo Americans. According to the 1960 Census, in the Southwest 66.9 percent of 16- and 17-year-old Mexican Americans, as against 83.6 percent of Anglo Americans of the same age, were enrolled in school. For those 18 and 19 years of age, the respective percentages were 33.2 and 43.3.[18]

The dropout problem is especially acute among Mexican Americans, but has not been studied sufficiently.

Only one pilot study is available on this subject and its main concern is the extent of the problem. This investigation, conducted in three high schools of Los Angeles, shows that, between 1955 and 1957, 31 percent of the Mexican Americans, as compared with 19 percent of the other students, dropped out of school before high school graduation.[19]

In trying to account for this high dropout rate, only bits of information exist from studies directed at other problems. Thus one analysis of attitudes toward education reports that Mexican American junior and senior high school students are more likely to consider dropping out of school as desirable than Anglo Americans, even when social class and I. Q. are held constant.[20] Another investigation, focused upon problems of health, brings out the Mexican Americans' tendency to leave school because of their embarrassment about being poorly dressed and having little spending money as compared with Anglo American students. The author of this study also refers to the feeling of scholastic inadequacy which characterizes Mexican American students, illustrating this reaction by quoting a university graduate who made the following comment about dropouts: "It was very hard for Mexican students . . . the teachers would run them down for being so dumb all the time. Most of them just got sick of it and dropped out of school." [21]

It remains to be seen to what extent the current national programs aimed at coping with the dropout problem in general will succeed in reducing the rate of dropouts among Mexican Americans. To summarize the situation as it exists now, Mexican American children are not prepared at home for the experiences which await them in school and the schools are not prepared or equipped to receive and hold these children.

Notes

1. Shannon and Krass, *op. cit.*, p. 223.

2. Thomas R. Garth and Harper D. Johnson, "The Intelligence and Achievement of Mexican Children in the U. S.," *Journal of Abnormal Social Psychology*, 29 (1934), p. 224; Nathaniel D. M. Hirsch, "A Study of Natio-Racial Mental Differences," *Genetic Psychology Monographs*, 1 (1926), p. 24; H. B. Carlson and N. Henderson, "The Intelligence of American Children of Mexican Parentage," *Journal of Abnormal Social Psychology*, 45 (1950), p. 548.

3. Heller, *op. cit.*, pp. 143-57.

4. James W. Vander Zanden, *American Minority Relations*, New York: Ronald Press, 1963, p. 231.

5. Horacio Ulibarri, "Teacher Awareness of Sociocultural Differences in Multicultural Classrooms," *Sociology and Social Research*, 45 (October, 1960), p. 52.

6. George I. Sanchez, *Forgotten People—A Study of New Mexicans*, Albuquerque: University of New Mexico Press, 1940, p. 327.

7. Louisa G. Sanchez, "The 'Latin-American' of the Southwest: Backgrounds and Curricular Implications." Unpublished Ph.D. dissertation, University of Texas, 1954. Pp. xviii, 208; McWilliams, *op. cit.*, p. 299; *Proceedings of the Conference on the Education of Spanish-Speaking People*, sponsored by the California State Department of Education, March, 1953, p. 20; Kluckhohn and Strodtbeck, *op. cit.*, pp. 250-1.

8. McWilliams, *op. cit.*, p. 299.

9. Thurston, *op. cit.*, p. 205.

10. Ulibarri, *op. cit.*, p. 55.

11. Thurston, *op. cit.*, p. 202.

12. "Interviews Given by the Panel on Values of Scholarships for Students of Mexican-American Ancestry," *Los Angeles School Journal*, 34 (April 2, 1951), p. 20.

13. *Proceedings, op. cit.*, p. 53.

14. Kluckhohn and Strodtbeck, *op. cit.*, pp. 250-1.

15. *Proceedings of the Conference on Educational Problems of Students of Mexican Descent*, Los Angeles: University of California, March 26, 1955, p. 28.

16. Heller, *op. cit.*, pp. 128-32, 143-57.

17. *Proceedings of the Conference on the Education of Spanish-Speaking People, op. cit.*, p. 30.

18. U. S. Bureau of Census; *Persons of Spanish Surname, op. cit.,* Table 4; State Volumes, Tables 94 and 101.

19. *Background for Planning, op. cit.,* p. 61.

20. George D. Demos, "Attitudes of Mexican-American and Anglo-American Groups toward Education," *Sociology and Social Research,* 46 (August, 1962), p. 255.

21. Clark, *op. cit.,* pp. 69-71.

FIVE

The Delinquents

School experiences generally tend to leave Mexican American children with the feeling that it is extremely difficult or impossible for them to acquire status within the school system. Evidence presented in the preceding chapter concerning scholastic problems and low I. Q. scores of Mexican American students makes it clear that status on the basis of scholarship is a rather rare achievement among Mexican Americans.

This unsatisfied status need may help to explain the exaggerated importance that Mexican American high school students attach to other sources of status, such as the paraphernalia accompanying graduation. Mexican American boys have spoken to me about their fears of not having enough money to buy these objects. "When you graduate, the senior luncheon, the sweater, the prom and other things cost about 200 dollars. Many boys figure that there is no use going on with school if you are not able to afford these things," explained one high school graduate. These things may seem very unimportant to an outsider compared with what the Mexican American forfeits if he does not graduate from high school. Only when one realizes how hungry for achieving respect in the eyes of their fellows these youngsters are can one grasp the importance which such symbols hold for them. Clothes, transistor radios, customized cars are not mere commodities—they serve as "guides to human worth." [1]

Of the theories that have been formulated to explain delinquent behavior, the one that seems to fit the case of Mexican American delinquency closest is the one put forth by Albert Cohen. He sees the delinquent subculture as the solution that lower class youth has evolved to the problems that prevail among them. According to him, "These problems are chiefly status problems: certain children are denied status in the respectable society because they cannot meet the criteria of the respectable status system." [2] The lower class boys are more likely than their middle class peers to find themselves at the bottom of the status hierarchy whenever they move in the middle class world, of which the school is an integral part.

The Mexican American boys are plagued with such problems on two scores: because they are largely of lower class background and because they belong to a low ranking ethnic minority. In addition, these problems may weigh more heavily on them than on their Anglo American peers because of their home socialization in the importance of honor and respect.

Gangs

Often the Mexican American boy finds the answer to his status problems in the gang. Beatrice Griffith perceived this when she wrote about the youngster who became a member of a gang:

> During his nine years of intermittent schooling, Chaco has one fact impressed on him. The only group that has meaning for him is his neighborhood group. It is not the school, where the "American" teachers tell him about a world in which he has no real part. . . . But in the neighborhood gang is the stuff of living as he knows it.[3]

No major sociological study of Mexican American gangs has yet been made, but those who have written about them generally speak of their great influence on Mexican American boys.[4] An extreme example is Carey McWilliams' statement that "a 'gang' of Mexican boys is held together by a set of associations so strong that they outweigh, or often outweigh, such influence as the home, the school, and the church."[5] This assertion is, however, supported by a recent study on behavior of adolescent boys associating in groups of their own choosing. In observing Mexican American boys (living in a Mexican neighborhood of a large city in Texas), the Sherifs found that when the boys had to decide between joining in a group activity and family obligation or church duties, going with the group was by far the more common decision.[6] This is especially noteworthy since family connections—including both the immediate family and related kin—are the most important social ties among Mexican American adults.

The findings by the Sherifs cited above concerned a nondelinquent group, but in this, as well as in other respects, the delinquent and nondelinquent groups in

Mexican neighborhoods are quite similar. What differentiates the delinquent from the nondelinquent ones is the degree of socially disapproved behavior. Mexican American boys generally tend to form neighborhood cliques to which they refer as *camaradas, amigos,* and in some parts of Texas as *palomillas.* The last means moths and alludes to the fact that youths, like moths clustering around a light, naturally move in groups. Mexican American adults hold that in such associations of male friends, in which the boy spends most of his free time, he becomes a man. Here he learns the terminology of sex and the techniques of dealing with girls. He also engages here in the game of verbal dueling and thus acquires verbal articulateness so valued in men.[7]

In addition to the degree of socially disapproved behavior, the delinquent associations differ from the rest in their claim of a territory that they feel bound to defend. In such a territory they tend to intimidate nondelinquents, who seem very careful not to antagonize them. An 18-year-old Mexican American boy explained recently in Los Angeles:

> A gang hangs around the corner just a block away from me. The leader of the gang likes my sister. I wasn't part of the gang but nobody would pick on me because the big boss liked my sister. If I would go out to the store, sometimes a guy would come up and ask, "Have a dime?" or something. They ask you for money because they want to buy cigarettes or something. You got to give it to them. . . . Sometimes you see in their eyes that they have been taking pills [narcotics] or something. You act friendly with them and you're better off giving them a quarter than having them jump you.

These gangs are often referred to as *pachuco* gangs and its members as *pachucos.* There is considerable controversy concerning the origin of this term which gained wide publicity in 1943, the time of the shameful "zoot suit" riots against Mexican Americans in Los Angeles.⁸ However, this term is now rarely used by Mexican American youth in Los Angeles. They call the delinquents *eses*, *batos*, and most often *cholos*. The first seems to have evolved from the common greeting form that delinquents use in addressing one another: "*Ay, ese*," "hey, you." *Batos* means guys, and George Barker traces the word to the Spanish dialect in New Mexico where its meaning is sweetheart.⁹ As for *cholos*, it is the term used in Mexico to designate Indians and people at the bottom of the social scale. We do not know whether these terms have spread out of Los Angeles. In some parts of New Mexico, *chuco*, a shortened version of *pachuco*, is gaining ground.

Their Speech and Dress

The above terms also illustrate the distinct speech of the delinquents, what Barker calls the "*Pachuco* argot." He thinks that it originated in El Paso and that the greatest single impetus to its spread came in 1942 when a large group of boys migrated from there to Los Angeles. It flourished in Los Angeles in the forties and has since extended over a considerable part of the Southwest in more or less attenuated form. Composed in part of Spanish, southwestern Spanish, and English words (like *ganga* for gang and *songa* for song), these are often given special and distinct meaning, as in the case of *batos*, noted above. *Suave*, which in Spanish means smooth, is one of the words that they use most frequently to denote approval. Thus, *esta suave* means it's fine, it's nice, it's swell. A large part of its vocabulary consists of new words, like the much used *orale* to mean O.K. Strange and sometimes comical to the outsider sound the literal Spanish trans-

lations of American slang which figure prominently in
this speech. Thus you have *agrar patada*, to get a kick
out of it, or *pintar el pizo en colorado*, to paint the
town red.[10] In its purest form, Munroe Edmonson
asserts, *Pachuco* is the only southwestern dialect which
is unintelligible to those speaking other Spanish dia-
lects.[11] However, I have never encountered a Mexican
American youth, living in a Mexican American neighborhood, to whom this speech was unintelligible. The
boys that I interviewed in Los Angeles—even the most
acculturated and mobility-oriented ones—did not think
of it as a separate language or dialect and objected to
its being designated as such. To quote one of them,
"It's just slang. Just like any other group, they [*cholos*]
have their slang." As Barker noted in Tucson in 1946
—and it still held true in Los Angeles in the summer
of 1965—many young Mexican Americans not only
understand *Pachuco*, or what could perhaps be re-
named the *Cholo* argot, but also use some of its expressions. This is similar to the speech pattern of
American youth in general as compared with its delinquents. To know some *Pachuco*, or *Cholo*, expressions
is a mark of sophistication among boys of Mexican
descent. The knowledge and use of such expressions
serves notice that the individual is modern and in step
with his own generation. This should not be taken to
mean that the nondelinquent youths, especially the
ambitious ones to be discussed in the next chapter,
speak the argot fluently. They seldom do for they tend
to refrain from it as habitual means of communication.[12] It is partly a conscious effort since they seem
bent on emphasizing that they are different from the
cholos. The habitual use by the latter of the argot as
a means of communication can be taken to mean, according to Barker, that its users are not interested in
rising socially.

More noticeable than the style of speech is the distinctive mode of dress of the gang members. The *pachuco* garb, the "zoot suit" (baggy trousers narrowing at the cuffs, with a long chain hanging from the pocket and a long draped coat), which had been widely publicized during the anti-Mexican Los Angeles riots of 1943, has been replaced by the bell-bottom pants or "khakis," split at the bottom, sported by the delinquents today. However, it seems that the Mexican American delinquents in Los Angeles are increasingly abandoning this distinct attire and "going continental" or "semi-continental," shifting to the current fashion fads of the nondelinquents. "Continental" refers to the following outfit: tight pants, tight jacket, pointed shoes, and pink socks. The less "dressed up" look is the "semi-continental": "continental" pants and regular shirt and shoes or a "continental" shirt and regular slacks and shoes. As a Mexican American youngster explained when trying to compare the *cholos* with other boys, "You can become continental in a matter of hours by dressing like a continental. One day you may be walking around just like a regular person, next day you are a continental."

The nondelinquent boys often credit female influence for the change in the *cholos*' attire. To quote from one of the interviews that illustrate it:

(He) I noticed recently with my generation that it's going out [*cholo* dress]. Most of the *cholos* that you do find are in the younger set, the younger kids, and most of the *cholos* who are seventeen and up are changing over. . . . Most of them are turning over to continental. They still dress in khakis but a lot of them are going in for dressing up a lot more. They are going in for style because a lot of girls are emphasizing style. A lot of girls are switching over from *cholos*; they are being more classy, they want more out of life, let's put it that way. And they won't go out with a guy if he's a *cholo*. They don't want to associate with *cholos*, yet they are, they come from a lower section of town. You can tell they are trying to improve a great deal, the way they dress. They can't get ahead as far as education is concerned. As far as styles go and finding a better job, they emphasize that. If a guy wants to associate with the girls, he has to go over to the other side.

(I) The other side in dress or in other ways, too?

(He) They still associate with the same crowd. They still do the same things but it's a cleaner crowd, they are more clean cut about it. They still do all the dropping [taking narcotics] and crime and stuff like this but there is great emphasis on clothes.

Their Activities

Separate Mexican American juvenile gangs are prominent in the cities heavily populated by members of this ethnic group. They even seem to attract and influence larger portions of Mexican American youth than do gangs in the majority lower class areas. Direct statistics are not available, but a recent empirical study supports this contention: with social class and I. Q. held constant, it shows that more Mexican American than Anglo American students, grade seven through twelve, approve of gangs.[13] A particular proneness to join gangs, if this in fact is the case, would not be difficult to explain. The conditions that have been attested as conducive to gang formation—such as sharp cultural differences, distance between youths and parents, living in slums—are operating in the case of Mexican Americans, and some of them to a greater degree than among other lower class groups.[14]

Similarly to dress, the Mexican American gangs seem to resemble the organizational forms and activities of Anglo American gangs. The common activities are:

holding smut sessions, dancing, drinking, gambling and narcotic drug parties; gang fighting, raiding, robbing, and committing acts of vandalism. Through these doings the participants seek and achieve status in delinquent society and a sense of enjoyment, "kicks." The dullness of the many hours spent "hanging around the corners" of the drab areas in which these youths live—and they often refer to it and complain about it —is relieved by the excitement of these events. In questioning some Mexican American delinquents on why they participated in such endeavors, the most frequent answer I received was "just for kicks."

But whether engaged in such activities or not, whether members of delinquent gangs or not, Mexican American boys in general perceive "getting in trouble with the police" as a natural state of affairs and "staying out of trouble" as a stroke of fortune. This could be illustrated by many examples but we shall confine ourselves to two. One of the most ambitious high school graduates that I interviewed, the president of his graduating class, who is 18 years old, had this to say:

> Mostly everybody gets in conflict with the police once in a while, whether it is a parking ticket, whether it is being arrested for drunk driving, for narcotics, or something else. You always seem to get caught at the other side of the thing. . . . I got into trouble once. It was right after the school dance. . . . I was going home and I think it was about four blocks from the dance that they pulled me over, a police car pulled us over and pulled guns on us. They opened my eyes and wanted to know whether I was on dope. I wanted to know what I did. They just said that there was a report of some activity, that some Mexican boys were taking dope, that there was a *cholo* party. So they opened my eyes and everything, rolled up my sleeve, whether I was taking dope. Then they said that I was

O.K. and let me go. But they had no reason for stopping me.

A 20-year-old youth, whose ambition is to be a probation officer and who goes to junior college in the evening, related:

> I've only been to jail once; I only got to the reception desk. It's far enough for me. I was taken in for questioning about two years ago when I was eighteen. . . . There were robberies in the neighborhood and they were picking everybody up.

Delinquency Rates

To what extent the high rate of Mexican American delinquency is an expression of the heavy policing of the areas where large numbers of Mexican Americans are concentrated has not as yet been ascertained. But the statistical fact of the high delinquency rate is well known, and even exaggerated in the cities of the Southwest. Especially since the 1943 "zoot suit" riots, noted above, delinquency has become synonymous with "Mexican" in the minds of many southwesterners.[15]

Slum life, generational strain, social discrimination, poor scholastic performance, numerous school dropouts, and prominent gang behavior—more characteristic of Mexican Americans than of Anglo Americans—strongly encourage a high delinquency rate. Among those who express concern about the marked delinquency of Mexican American youth, two extreme positions predominate. There are those who simply equate delinquency with Mexican descent, and there are their opponents who admit, albeit reluctantly, the higher rate of Mexican American delinquency but hold our society solely responsible for it. The former focus on the supposedly negative characteristics of Mexicans, while the latter stress the unjust limitations our society has imposed upon members of this group.

What are the known facts concerning Mexican American delinquency?

No general study has been conducted on the subject, but a few investigations of particular communities exist. One of the most recent of these is the Los Angeles study of 1957-8,[16] which is based on the Los Angeles Probation Department statistics, considered by experts in the field among the best in the country as to scope and reliability. The following discussion will rely heavily upon this study which used 1956 statistics because by 1958 there was not only a record of all the cases that came to the attention of the Probation Department but also of the disposition of each case. It should be added that implicit in our discussion is the conventional definition of delinquency as behavior among children and youths in violation of the law.[17]

As slight reflection would indicate, but contrary to some prejudiced views, the majority of delinquents in the Southwest are not Mexican Americans and the great majority of Mexican American youth are not delinquent. Thus, for example, in Los Angeles County, about 80 percent of the juveniles referred to the Los Angeles County Probation Department in 1956 were not Mexican Americans.[18]

Still, the rate of offenses in this group is higher than among non-Mexican "whites." In fact, according to the Los Angeles study, their rate exceeds that of Negroes in the same county. But these statistical facts should be placed in a balanced perspective. The ethnic differentials in delinquency rates, although sizable, are not as pronounced as age and sex differentials. This is to say that, in predicting the likelihood of children becoming delinquent, it is more important to know their sex and age than to know their ethnic background. Nevertheless, the social and sociological problem remains of explaining the comparative prevalence of delinquency among Mexican Americans.

Explanation of High Delinquency

The following three explanations (among others) for the high rate of delinquency among Mexican Americans and racial minorities in general have been set forth in social science literature.

1. Mexican Americans are "highly visible" and their rates are an expression of differential "pick up" by the police.

2. Minority group status as such produces a high rate of delinquency.

3. High rates are due to frustrations produced by discrimination.[19] (Although it figures in the literature as a separate explanation, logically (3) could be considered as one of the many possible specifications of (2).)

The inadequacy of these explanations becomes apparent by introducing the case of the Japanese Americans. They, like the Mexican Americans, are subject to the three conditions outlined above, and yet their rates are the lowest of all racial groups, including those of the majority whites, whose rate is about double that of the Japanese Americans.[20]

It is also argued that the high incidence of delinquency among Mexican Americans is simply a reflection of the fact that they are predominantly lower class, for this class in general is known to have a high rate of delinquency.[21] (The logic behind this argument takes the following form: in calculating the rate of delinquents per 10,000 youths of Mexican descent, we actually obtain almost the rate per 10,000 youths of lower class origin; on the other hand, when we calculate the rate of delinquents per 10,000 Anglo Americans, we obtain a reduced rate because a good portion of these 10,000 are middle and upper class youths.) Unquestionably, there is much to this argument since, as has been previously shown, the Mexican American population occupies predominantly lower socioeconomic positions and is markedly underrepresented in middle class occupations. Is the class difference, however, large enough to explain, for example, the more than triple rate of referrals to the Probation Department of juveniles of Mexican descent in Los Angeles County, as compared with Anglo Americans (170.5 and 54.4 per 10,000 juveniles, respectively, in 1956)? [22] We do not have the necessary figures to estimate how much of the difference between the rates in this case is due to differential class distribution. Moreover, there appear to be no studies of Mexican American delinquency in which the factor of class is held constant. But census data on occupational and educational distribution of Mexican Americans in urban areas indicate that class alone does not explain the large difference between this group and Anglo Americans. The two groups differ less in the ratio of their lower classes than in the ratio of delinquents in their youth populations. Thus the problem remains: what is the ethnic factor in Mexican American juvenile delinquency?

Is it family disorganization, so frequently cited as of major importance in stimulating juvenile delinquency? This factor has been stressed by many students since W. I. Thomas and Florian Znaniecki, several decades ago, documented the association between disorganization of the family among Polish immigrants and youth criminality.[23] However, in the case of Mexican Americans we have no reason to believe that the family is in sharp decline. On the contrary, as brought out earlier, the evidence points to its continuity along traditional lines.

As shown by the Los Angeles statistics, families of Mexican American and Anglo American juvenile offenders do not differ significantly in the proportion of homes broken by marital discord—27 and 29 percent, respectively. A more detailed analysis reveals that Mexican Americans exceed Anglo Americans in the proportion of offenders whose parents have been separated or were never married; but this difference is almost balanced by an overrepresentation of divorced parents in the Anglo American group. The Mexican Americans, however, differ substantially from the Anglo Americans in containing a higher percentage of orphaned youths. In this respect, they resemble Negro offenders, a similarity that reflects the lower life-expectancy of both the Mexican American and the Negro populations.[24]

What appears to have more bearing on the delinquency problem is the fact that the Mexican American community has almost no welfare agencies of its own. The large numbers of the group's offenders referred to the police and the probation departments may be, in part, a reflection of this fact. On this score, the Mexican American community differs sharply from the Jewish and Japanese American communities. At the same time, the general welfare agencies that operate in areas of high Mexican American concentration are held in low regard and are often shunned. The proverbial interviews by social workers are especially distasteful to Mexican Americans because they seem to violate their sense of shame, *pena*, and sense of honor. Their attitude is similar to that which William Foote Whyte found among the Italian Americans in Boston.[25] Mexican Americans, therefore, illustrate Sophia Robison's argument that the high delinquency rates of certain groups are substantially influenced by the absence of the kind of welfare agencies that certain other ethnic groups with low rates, notably the Jews, maintain and which assume responsibility for many problem cases that would otherwise go through official channels.[26] The lack of such agencies among Mexican Americans in all likelihood contributes to their reported high delinquency rate, but even if allowance is made for this variable, a rate differential still remains.[27]

Clearly, this differential is in part a product of the fact that Mexican Americans in urban centers tend to cluster in areas of physical deterioration, congested population, and economic dependency—the kind of neighborhoods in which delinquency flourishes. It has been shown that minority groups with high delinquency rates, such as the Polish Americans of Chicago and the Negroes of Baltimore, when divided in terms of lower rent and higher rent areas, show significantly higher delinquency rates in the lower rental areas.[28] Although this kind of breakdown has not been reported for Mexican Americans, their conspicuous concentration in very deteriorated neighborhoods strongly suggests the salience of this ecological situation.

Thus several mutually reinforcing circumstances are at work in bringing about a particularly high incidence of delinquency among Mexican Americans. These include overrepresentation in the lower class, acute status deprivation, heavy concentration in slum areas, lack of group-oriented welfare agencies, which are especially noticeable, and no doubt other factors not caught up in this introductory study.

Male-Female Differences in Delinquency Rates

In the Southwest one can often hear the remark that, although delinquency is prominent among Mexican American boys, it is rarer among Mexican American, than among Anglo American, girls. Such comments are usually accompanied by references to the strict upbringing and supervision of Mexican American girls. This association sometimes appears in scholarly works; for example, Ruth Tuck writes: "Say what you will about the cloistering of girls, it has a positive effect on delinquency statistics. Practically no Mexican American girl is ever arrested by the police." [29]

Whatever the situation in the past, there is evidence that now delinquency is not that uncommon among Mexican American females, but then the "cloistered" girl may be the rarity among them today. While Mexican American delinquency conforms to the general pattern by being much more prominent among males than among females, there actually exists a higher rate of delinquency among Mexican American, than among Anglo American, girls, at least in the Los Angeles area. (But, in contrast to male delinquency, there is less delinquency among Mexican American girls than among Negro girls.) The difference between the male and female rates, however, is higher among Mexican Americans (ratio: 620) than among Anglo Americans (ratio: 370).[30] Thus, for every delinquent girl there are six delinquent boys among Mexican Americans but less than four boys among Anglo Americans.

These findings are consistent with the generalization of Sutherland and Cressey that the male-female ratio in crime is directly related to the relative social standing of males and females in the society or group being examined.[31] But they are not consistent with the explanation put forth by Talcott Parsons. Parsons holds that males in our society have a higher rate of delinquency than females because, in the process of acquiring masculine role identity, boys react against the feminine identification of their childhood by engaging in behavior marked by "compulsive masculinity." [32] But among Mexican Americans, boys from early childhood on tend to identify with the father or grown males in the family and not with the mother.[33] In this case, then, and perhaps in others (notably, Puerto Ricans[34]), the offenses the Mexican American boys commit are in some ways consistent with the male sex role which they learn from early childhood on. What may contribute to the higher rate of male delinquency among Mexican Americans is the disturbed father-adolescent son relationship. As was shown earlier, this is largely due to the son's threatening or usurping the authority of the father.

From the above discussion of total rates, we proceed to a comparison of specific offenses of Mexican Americans and Anglo Americans. Although many studies of delinquency of particular minority groups confine themselves to an analysis of total rates, we propose that additional understanding of the Mexican American pattern is gained from shifting our focus to the nature of offenses.

Nature of Offenses

In examining the distribution of specific offenses among Mexican Americans (see Table 3), we can readily see that similarities outweigh the differences between their pattern and that of Anglo Americans. (This similarity is rarely stressed in discussions of juvenile delinquency among ethnic groups.)

Illegitimate sex relations are the principal offense among Mexican American as well as Anglo American girls, and—in a strikingly similar proportion—26 and 28 percent of the total offenses, respectively. The second most frequent offense for both groups is runaway, 20 and 18 percent, respectively. Charges of incorrigibility rank third, 13 percent of the total Mexican American, and 16 percent of the total Anglo American, female offenses. Surprisingly, the offenses which appear in a higher proportion among the Mexican American girls are the acts that are usually associated with the male rather than the female role, namely, assault and battery, petty theft, and auto theft.

The pattern of offenses among boys of Mexican descent also resembles that of the majority youth. (See

Table 3 PERCENTAGE DISTRIBUTION OF MALE JUVENILES RE-
FERRED TO THE LOS ANGELES COUNTY PROBATION DEPARTMENT,
BY TYPE OF OFFENSE: 1956

Type of Offense	Anglo American (N—4219)	Mexican American (N—1582)
Against Persons		
Homicide	.2	.4
Robbery	2.2	3.2
Assault-Battery	2.7	8.2
Forcible Rape	.3	.7
Against Property		
Burglary	18.7	10.7
Grand Theft	1.0	.5
Petty Theft	9.1	7.2
Auto Theft	20.5	17.1
Other Theft	1.1	.8
Forgery	.3	.1
Against Public Morality— *Major Offenses*		
Illegitimate Sex Relations	3.0	3.5
Homosexual Acts	1.4	.6
Other Sex Acts	1.9	.7
Narcotic Offenses	4.3	14.1
Liquor Laws—Violations	2.4	3.2
Against Public Morality— *Minor Offenses*		
Disorderly Conduct	1.9	3.7
Incorrigibility	3.6	2.5
Malicious Mischief	2.7	1.5
Runaway	2.0	1.9
Transiency	2.4	.9
Truancy	3.1	1.5
Vagrancy	2.6	3.8
Weapons	1.3	2.7
Improper Companions	.2	.3
Other Specific Violations	1.3	1.4
Traffic Violations	9.8	8.8
TOTAL	100.0%	100.0%

SOURCE: Special Release, Los Angeles Probation Department,
1957.

Table 3.) That Mexican Americans are fully acculturated to the "car complex" is reflected in the fact that
auto theft is their leading offense, as it is among Anglo
Americans. (Like the latter, Mexican American boys ac-
cused of car theft often plead that their intention was
not to steal but to borrow the car for a "joy ride.")

Some Mexican American boys whom I interviewed
held the girls ultimately responsible for car thefts and
thefts connected with payments on cars. A 19-year-old
boy, for example, gave the following answer to the
question: "What makes a shining new car so important?"

> As far as that is concerned it's the girls who are set-
> ting the pace. . . . Some girls told me that the only
> reason they go with certain guys is that they have a
> nice car. When I go with a girl I make it clear that we
> will double-date because I don't have a car. If they
> want to go, fine, and if they don't that's fine, too. . . .
> There are guys who go way out; they can't afford it
> but they get a car and before you know it, they come,
> jack it up, and take it away. A lot of guys I know have
> received stolen goods just to make the car payments.
> They get a percentage out of it and they do it. Say a
> 200 dollar T.V., they'd sell it for 50 bucks to make
> the car payment. When they get the car they don't
> think of this. They go into it and say "I'll work it
> out." But when they find themselves in a bind, they say
> "just once." But if they do it once [steal or sell stolen
> goods], they do it twice and they go on doing it.

Besides car theft, the other major offenses among
both Mexican American and Anglo American boys are
petty theft, burglary, and traffic violations. If delin-
quencies are grouped into conventional categories, as
in Table 3, offenses against property constitute the
largest category for both Mexican American and Anglo
American boys. Of offenses against persons, homicide

and forcible rape constitute the smallest proportions in both groups.

One major difference between these groups is the substantially larger proportion of assault and battery (8.2 percent for Mexican Americans, as compared with 2.7 percent for Anglo Americans). A second striking contrast is the high percentage of narcotic offenses among Mexican Americans, which is more than three times that of Anglo Americans. On the other hand, there is a substantially smaller proportion of burglary among Mexican Americans (10.7 compared with 18.7 percent for Anglo Americans). High rates of assault and battery and the low rate of burglary are perhaps reflections of the previously discussed values of manliness and honor.[35] To consider himself a man, the Mexican American must be ready to fight to protect his and his family's honor. In contrast, burglary is considered cowardly, for a man's honor requires that he confront his adversary.

Honor as a valued male characteristic is only rivaled by adventurousness and enjoyment of life. The higher rate of narcotic offenses among Mexican Americans may reflect a desperate search for excitement in surroundings, especially the neighborhood and school, which is found to be drab and void of excitement. As noted in Chapter Four, education in our school system tends to be treated as a means for achieving economic success and not as the source of excitement and adventure that it might be.

Some awareness of the significance of narcotics in their lives is gained from their songs. Here, for example, is part of a *Pachuco* song, in its original and in English translation. In the preceding lines a father warns his son not to fight, he refuses to obey, is wounded and utters these last words before he dies:

Lo que le encargue a mi jefe
Que no me entierre en Califa

Que me entierre en Arizona
Con tres costales de grifa

My last words to my father
Were that they bury me not in Califa (California)
But that I be buried in Arizona
With three sacks of marijuana[36]

But the easier access to narcotics, because of their
flow from Mexico and of the adult contacts that Mexican American boys have there, must not be overlooked
as a factor in the higher rate of narcotic offenses.[37] In
probing about this problem, we got a number of responses from Mexican American boys, of which the following is typical:

Strangely enough a lot of them get hooked in Ti-
juana [a town just across the border from California].
They go there for a visit; I don't know whether I
should tell you this. A lot of them, to put it bluntly,
look for excitement, kicks, and they figure they will
get it in T. J. [Tijuana]. Next thing, you know, they're
trying the stuff. They get a kick out of it. Pretty soon
they want to push everybody else on it, they say, "I'll
give you some," "I'll let you try some." That is another reason why many Mexican Americans are put
down.

Some of the boys who are not narcotic users related
that they have been repeatedly invited to try but that
they are determined to resist. Among them is a 17-year-
old boy who had this to say:

A person once told me, about a year ago, that I am
chicken. I says, well it doesn't bother me what you're
saying. The only way I would take it is if they tied me
and shoved it down my throat. . . . I've seen what it
does to people. Where I was raised [East Los Angeles],
where my grandmother lives, there are a lot of narcotic users. I know a lot of people who take narcotics.

If you really want to, you can start on this kick but most of my good friends have never touched it. The others, they are your friends—you went to school with them and you say hello to them. Just because they take the stuff you can't stop saying hello to them. I talk to them. I don't get involved with them though. When I see him at a party I will say hello and talk to him but I wouldn't go out together. . . . At school they come up and say, "Would you like to buy some stuff?" I say, "I have no money," "I don't want it," or "I don't take the stuff."

(I)   When you have so many boys taking it, isn't it a temptation?

(He)   I've seen what it does to people. I had a cousin on my father's side who was hooked. I've seen him shake pretty bad. . . .

More often, however, nonusers tell of users warning them to stay away from drugs. As a recent high school graduate told me:

They don't make it attractive. They make it sound bad. They tell you, "You're a good kid, you're young, you'll get into a lot of trouble." Pretty soon they make it sound like you're really not a man, that you can't take it. But yet they are giving you the straight dope on it. They tell you, "Don't take it, you're a little kid, I don't want you to get sick on it." After a while you start saying to yourself, "I won't get sick. Just once." You want to feel like a man. Soon you're on it.

In concluding this chapter, it may be suggested that the excess of juvenile delinquents among Mexican Americans—the number that remains after class and the other factors discussed above are held constant—is not composed of deviants from the cultural pattern of the Mexican American population but rather of boys who overconform to this pattern. In this view, the most striking "deviants" among Mexican American youth are not these delinquents but the youngsters, to be discussed in the next chapter, who aspire to or who do attend college.

Notes

1. Julia and Herman Schwendinger, "Delinquent Stereotypes of Probable Victims," Part II, Unpublished paper, School of Criminology, University of California, Berkeley, p. 19.

2. Albert K. Cohen, *Delinquent Boys—The Culture of the Gang*, Glencoe: The Free Press, 1955, especially pp. 119-21.

3. Griffith, *op. cit.*, pp. 43-44.

4. To list some of them: E. S. Bogardus, "Mexican-American Youth and Gangs," *Sociology and Social Research*, 28 (September, 1943), pp. 55-66; Sam Glane, "Juvenile Gangs in East Los Angeles," *Focus* (September, 1950), pp. 136-41; Griffith, *op. cit.*; E. M. Lemert and Judy Rosberg, "Crime and Punishment among Minority Groups in Los Angeles County," *Proceedings of the Pacific Coast Sociological Society* (June, 1946), pp. 133-45; McWilliams, *op. cit.*, p. 239.

5. McWilliams, *ibid.*

6. Sherif, *op. cit.*, p. 29.

7. William Madsen, *The Mexicans of South Texas*, New York: Holt, Rinehart and Winston, 1965, pp. 53-56.

8. Ralph H. Turner and Samuel J. Surace, "Zoot-suiters and Mexicans: Symbols in Crowd Behavior," *American Journal of Sociology*, 62 (July, 1956), pp. 14-20.

9. George C. Barker, *Pachuco, an American-Spanish Argot and Its Social Functions in Tucson, Arizona*, Tucson: University of Arizona Press, Social Science Bulletin, 21, No. 18, p. 5.

10. *Ibid.*

11. Edmonson, *op. cit.*, p. 16.

12. Barker, *Pachuco . . .* , *op. cit.*, pp. 17-23.

13. Demos, *op. cit.*, p. 255.

14. Walter M. Miller, "Lower Class Culture as a Generating Milieu of Gang Delinquency," *Journal of Social Issues*, 14 (1958), pp. 5-19.

15. N. D. Humphrey, "The Stereotype and Social Types of Mexican-American Youths," *Journal of Social Psychology*, 22 (1945), p. 69.

16. Celia Stopnicka Heller, "The Pattern of Offenses among

Juveniles of Mexican Descent," paper presented at the annual meeting of the Pacific Sociological Association, Tucson, Arizona, April, 1961; Joseph Eaton and Kenneth Polk, *Measuring Delinquency*, Pittsburgh: University of Pittsburgh Press, 1961.

17. Edwin H. Sutherland and Donald H. Cressey, *Principles of Criminology*, Philadelphia: Lippincott, 1960, pp. 203-6.

18. Heller, "The Pattern of Offenses . . . ," *op. cit.*, p. 3.

19. Simpson and Yinger, *op. cit.*, pp. 456-60; Sutherland and Cressey, *op. cit.*, p. 147.

20. Sutherland and Cressey, *ibid.*, p. 138.

21. Simpson and Yinger, *op. cit.*, p. 57; Griffith, *op. cit.*, p. 203.

22. Heller, "The Pattern of Offenses . . . ," *op. cit.*, p. 5.

23. W. I. Thomas and Florian Znaniecki, *The Polish Peasant in Europe and America*, Vol. V, Boston: Gorham, 1920, p. 344.

24. Heller, "The Pattern of Offenses . . . ," *op. cit.*, p. 7.

25. William Foote Whyte, *Street Corner Society*, Chicago: University of Chicago Press, 1955, p. 104.

26. Sophia M. Robison, *Can Delinquency Be Measured?* New York: Columbia University Press, 1936.

27. See, e.g.: Sutherland and Cressey, *op. cit.*, p. 159; Marshall B. Clinard, "Sociologists and American Criminology," *Journal of Criminal Law*, 4 (January, 1951), p. 567.

28. Sutherland and Cressey, *op. cit.*, pp. 158-63; Clifford R. Shaw and Henry D. McKay, *Juvenile Delinquency in Urban Areas*, Chicago: University of Chicago Press, 1942; Bernard Lander, *Toward an Understanding of Juvenile Delinquency*, New York: Columbia University Press, 1954, p. 32.

29. Tuck, *op. cit.*, p. 214.

30. Heller, "The Pattern of Offenses . . . ," *op. cit.*, p. 12.

31. Sutherland and Cressey, *op. cit.*, pp. 111-5.

32. Talcott Parsons, *Essays in Sociological Theory*, Glencoe: The Free Press, 1949, pp. 257-9.

33. Tuck, *op. cit.*, p. 124; Burma, *op. cit.*, p. 11.

34. Elena Padilla, *Up from Puerto Rico*, New York: Columbia University Press, 1958.

35. Perhaps the finding that Mexican American delinquent boys, in contrast to girls, show significantly more hostility than Anglo American delinquent boys (when tested on the Manifest Hostility Scale) could also be interpreted in this manner. For a description of the study that came out with this finding, see Don L. Swickard and Bernard Spilka, "Hostility Expression Among

Delinquents of Minority and Majority Groups," *Journal of Consulting Psychology*, 25 (June, 1961), pp. 216-220.

36. Barker, *Pachuco* . . . , *op. cit.*, p. 30.

37. Heller, "The Pattern of Offenses . . . ," *op. cit.*, p. 12.

SIX

The Ambitious

Much like delinquent behavior, lack of ambition is a stereotype widely linked in the Southwest with the image of Mexican Americans in general and Mexican American youth in particular. Just as, in the minds of some, delinquency is synonymous with Mexican descent, ambition is held to be antithetical to it. This may perhaps partly account for the fact that until recently social scientists have been little concerned with the occupational motivation of Mexican American *youth*, although some writers have commented on the low occupational goals and achievements of Mexican Americans in general.

Recall the Bogue finding cited earlier, to the effect that, among all ethnic groups in the United States, the Mexican American is the only one whose members do not show an intergenerational rise in socioeconomic status.[1] Add to it the comment by Ossie Simmons that there is "no motivation to mobility in the occupational structure since equivalent satisfactions are obtained from sources within the Mexican American group." [2] In light of this finding and this interpretation, what can now be said on the basis of recent, if limited, empirical studies assumes special significance here. For it seems clear that there are some Mexican American youths who, if they could fulfill their aspirations and expectations, would substantially exceed their parental generation in occupational and educational status.[3]

How large this sector is cannot be stated with precision. However, a useful single indicator appears to be high school graduation, which separates those who are beginning to have a claim upon the American dream from those who are not. On the basis of calculating the proportion of high school graduates in the 20- to 24-year age category, we estimate that this "ambitious" sector ranges from 25 percent of the total male Mexican American youth population in Texas to 38 percent in California.[4]

Mobility Aspirations

But are these boys, of whom there are about 40,000, ages 15 to 19, in the Southwest (according to the above method of calculation) ambitious in the conventional sense? Do their expectations exceed the achievements of their fathers? Affirmative answers to these questions are suggested by the Los Angeles study, for example, which shows that only 4 percent of the Mexican American male high school seniors expected to be in unskilled or semiskilled occupations, whereas 42 percent of their fathers worked in such occupations. Conversely, two percent of the fathers were in professions or semiprofessions, but as many as 35 percent of the sons aspired to such occupations. Findings of this kind, of course, should not obscure the fact that the aspirational level of Mexican American youths, even those who manage to become high school seniors, is substantially below that of Anglo American youths in general. However, when the class factor is controlled, Mexican Americans differ only to a small extent, mainly in that more of them expect to be skilled workers and fewer anticipate professional status.[5] As Ruth Tuck has observed, among Mexican Americans the professions may be the "preferred occupations" but "the realistic young are beginning to think that a skilled occupation might be a better bet." [6]

Since education constitutes an important means of realizing occupational ambitions, it is significant that the Los Angeles study shows many Mexican American male high school seniors expecting to exceed substantially the educational level of the parental generation. Merely five percent of their fathers attended college, but 44 percent among them expect to do so. (Similar figures on occupational and educational aspirations were obtained by Arturo De Hoyos in his study of Mexican American youth in Lansing, Michigan.[7]) Again, however, as in the case of occupational aspirations, the Mexican American boys had lower educational aspirations than their Anglo American fellow students. But when class is held constant, the differences shrink to a point where their significance is questionable.[8]

With respect to one type of occupation, the Los Angeles study shows that the Mexican American high school seniors do not differ from the majority in their ambition to be in business for themselves. This may be of special significance in light of the assertions by sociologists that, with the growth of large-scale organization, small business ownership has lost some of its meaning as a path of mobility.[9] Can it be that as this "much cherished ideal" is losing ground among the young Anglo Americans, especially of working class background, it is gaining ground among Mexican American youth? This trend, if it be such, might explain the similarity in the rate of Mexican American and Anglo American youth who expect to own their business or practice. It may also be the case that these third- and fourth-generation Americans of Mexican descent are showing a pattern similar to that displayed by some ethnic groups, such as the Jews, in the first generation. (The mobility path of many immigrant Jews was to leave the factory and establish a small business.[10])

One should also note the intensity of the ambitions of these boys, especially in view of the stereotyped image of Mexican Americans as a lackadaisical people with the "mañana" spirit. Over 90 percent of the high school seniors in the Los Angeles study answered that they would *not* consider themselves "successful enough" to relax their efforts as long as they were only "doing well enough to stay in the occupation" which is their lifework. About one third of these said that they would *never* consider themselves successful enough to relax their efforts, and the rest answered that they would relax only when doing as well or better than the average person in their occupation.[11] These relatively well-educated young Mexican Americans, then, display at least some of the attributes of typical achievers.

Achievement Values

Moreover, not only do these high school seniors resemble their Anglo American peers of the same social class in mobility goals but also in the endorsement of other values related to success. Among these are emphasis on hard work, "toughness" in pursuit of success, willingness to give up something valuable to achieve it, and a readiness to try new ways and to defer gratification.[12] This is especially noteworthy in light of the nature of their home socialization (see Chapter Three), which is largely devoid of these values. Consider, for example, their endorsement of deferred gratification. The home environment of Mexican Americans is saturated with a present-time orientation. Even the Mexican Americans in Racine, Wisconsin (who may be said to be mobility-oriented in some degree, having migrated from the Southwest in search of a better life), were found to be considerably less future-oriented than Anglo American immigrants in the same community. A much greater proportion of Mexican Americans (45 percent) than of Anglo Americans (14 percent) agreed that "a wise person lives for today and lets tomorrow take care of itself." [13] But in the Los Angeles study, significantly fewer Mexican American boys (class was controlled in both investigations) expressed preference for being "Someone who doesn't let his plans for the future keep him from enjoying the present." Over half of these respondents chose the second alternative, that of preferring to be "Someone who doesn't mind giving up all of his pleasure now so that he can be sure of the future." [14] Thus the Mexican American high school seniors, at least in response to questions of this type, showed themselves even more in favor of deferred gratification than their Anglo American peers.

The commitment to change on the part of many of these young people is also noteworthy, particularly since Mexican Americans have been characterized as belonging to one of those ethnic groups which "cling tenaciously to their own way of life." [15] The findings of the two empirical studies which contain information on the Mexican Americans' attitudes toward change are consistent with each other in demonstrating that at least a sector of the youth group is favorably disposed toward change: the De Hoyos study indicates that Mexican American youths have a positive general attitude toward change; and the Los Angeles investigation shows that they are as committed, in terms of endorsement of change, as are their Anglo American peers.[16]

Thus it is safe to say that there is a sizable percentage of Mexican American youth with values differing from and goals exceeding those of their fathers, which are quite similar to both the goals and the values of the majority youth. On the basis of available knowledge, we think that these mobility-oriented youths constitute a smaller proportion of the total Mexican American youth population than does the proportion of similarly ambitious youngsters among working class Anglo Americans. But even if these percentages were about the same, this would not spell the solution of the main status problem of the Mexican American minority.

The Pattern of Ethnic Mobility

Since recent immigrants generally (there have been minor exceptions), irrespective of country of origin, concentrate at the bottom of the socioeconomic ladder,[17] they must at some point in their history exceed the aspirations of the majority population of the same class if they are to take the leap which would enable them to approximate, or to surpass, the class distribution of the majority population. If they simply advanced to the same degree as those of similar socioeconomic status in the majority group, the gap between their class distribution and that of the majority population would continue.[18] And yet we know that some ethnic groups have outstripped the older generations of "native" Americans in achieving economic, if not social, success.[19]

Among many ethnic minorities, the process of moving toward the occupational distribution of the majority population starts with the second generation. Among others it begins later. And among a few—such as the Jews and the Japanese—this development is noted in the first generation.[20] In spite of these differences, however, members of almost all ethnic groups have eventually responded to the American ideology of advancement. The only large exception until now appears to be the Mexican Americans. But as we have shown, recent studies suggest that the Mexican Americans are now entering—to borrow Walt W. Rostow's term—the "take off stage" of social mobility.

Factors of Ambition

This new trend manifests itself in the mobility aspirations and values of one segment of Mexican American youth. The acceleration of this trend may depend in part on the diffusion of established information concerning the conditions conducive to stimulating the "achievement syndrome" among Mexican Americans. Unfortunately, such knowledge is very limited—in fact, no study has been specifically designed for this purpose. However, our secondary analysis of Turner's Los Angeles data sought to discover the principal variables in Mexican American ambition.

In this investigation it was found that Mexican American youngsters did not differ significantly in mobility goals and values along standard sociological variables. Neither the parents' occupation, education, country of birth, or the size of the family seemed to matter in the mobility orientation of the sons. In other words, among the boys whose parents were born in the United States, whose fathers had a higher occupation and education, or among boys who came from smaller families, the rate of ambitious youths was *not* higher than among the rest.[21] Perhaps the lack of differentiation among the first three variables—parental occupation, education, and country of birth—is simply a reflection of the homogeneity of the Mexican American population, discussed in Chapter Two. The occupational and educational differences in the boys' background may be too small to influence their ambitions. Similarly, the difference between the degree of acculturation of parents born in the United States and those born in Mexico may be too slight to affect the ambitions of their sons.

Of the several variables examined in this study, school integration stands out as the most salient factor associated with ambition: analysis of the Los Angeles data shows a significantly larger ratio of Mexican American boys in integrated schools who aspire to nonmanual occupations than in nonintegrated schools.[22] This may be quite an important finding in view of the fact that Mexican Americans are at present employed predominantly in manual occupations. It suggests that whether or not Mexican Americans will move toward the occupational distribution of the population at large will be partially determined by the continuation or the elimination of the school ghettos to which their children are presently confined. This finding also suggests that the *quality* of the school experience may be the decisive factor in stimulating ambition among Mexican American youth.

But the spread of ambition as such, it should be stressed, is not the only problem facing this group. For goals without avenues of realization create additional difficulties. The fact that there are Mexican American youths who resemble the majority in their mobility aspirations does not imply that they reach, or will reach, the same occupational positions as the majority youth. There are special obstacles that face Mexican Americans in the pursuit of their mobility goals—to which we turn in the following chapter.

Notes

1. Bogue, *op. cit.*, p. 372.

2. Simmons, *op. cit.*, p. 261.

3. Celia Stopnicka Heller, "Background and Ambition of Male Mexican-American High School Seniors in Los Angeles," paper presented at the annual meeting of the American Sociological Association, Los Angeles, California, 1963; Arturo De Hoyos, "Occupational and Educational Levels of Mexican-American Youth." Unpublished Ph.D. dissertation, Michigan State University, 1961; Peterson, *op. cit.*, pp. 25, 28.

4. Calculations based on 1960 Census figures in Table 7, *Persons of Spanish Surname, op. cit.*

5. Heller, "Background and Ambition of Male Mexican-American High School Seniors . . . ," *op. cit.*, p. 11; Demos, *op. cit.*

6. Tuck, *op. cit.*, p. 136.

7. De Hoyos, *op. cit.*, p. 76.

8. Heller, "Background and Ambition of Male Mexican-American High School Seniors . . . ," *op. cit.*, pp. 10-11.

9. See, e.g.: Lipset and Bendix, *op. cit.*, p. 173.

10. Fred L. Strodtbeck, "Jewish and Italian Immigration and Subsequent Status Mobility," in David C. McClelland, *Talent and Society*, Princeton, N. J.: Van Nostrand, 1958, p. 263.

11. From question 47 in Questionnaire by Ralph H. Turner. See: Turner, *The Social Context of Ambition, op. cit.*, p. 240.

12. Heller, "Ambitions of Mexican-American Youth . . . ," *op. cit.*, pp. 189-232.

13. Shannon and Krass, *op. cit.*, p. 227.

14. Heller, "Ambitions of Mexican-American Youth . . . ," *op. cit.*, p. 200.

15. Kluckhohn and Strodtbeck, *op. cit.*, p. 26.

16. De Hoyos, *op. cit.*, p. 94; Heller, "Ambitions of Mexican-American Youth . . . ," *op. cit.*, p. 222.

17. See, e.g.: Oscar Handlin, "Historical Perspectives of the American Ethnic Group," *Daedalus* (Spring, 1961), p. 228.

18. Celia Stopnicka Heller, "Class as an Explanation of Ethnic Differences in Mobility Aspirations—the Case of Mexican Americans," paper presented at the annual meeting of the Eastern Sociological Society, New York, 1965.

19. See, e.g.: Bernard Rosen, "Race, Ethnicity, and the Achievement Syndrome," *op. cit.*, p. 47.

20. Nathan Glazer, "Social Characteristics of American Jews, 1654-1954," in Morris Fine, ed., *American Year Book*, Philadelphia: Jewish Publication Society of America, 1955, pp. 32-33; William Caudill and George de Vos, "Achievement, Culture and Personality: The Case of Japanese Americans," *American Anthropologist*, 58 (1956), pp. 1102-26.

21. Heller, "Ambitions of Mexican-American Youth . . . ," *op. cit.*, pp. 90-102.

22. *Ibid.*, pp. 96-8.

SEVEN

Obstacles to Upward Mobility

Whether or not Mexican American youth will follow the pattern of its mobility-oriented sector, and in this way lay claim to the American Dream, largely depends on the extent to which the ambitious will be able to realize that Dream. The obstacles to its realization lie mainly in the realm of means and opportunities for advancement.

In this connection, mobility-oriented boys occupy an especially strategic position in influencing the future course of the Mexican American minority. They may become (in sociological language) "the positive-reference individuals," that is, the models of success for other Mexican American youth, if a substantial number prove themselves to be successful. But there is also the distinct possibility that they may become negative-reference individuals, for in the event that many of them should fail they would serve as a living reminder of the futility, frustration, and disenchantment that await Mexican Americans who allow themselves to be lured by the American Dream.

Deficiency in Resources

The latter danger is considerable because, first of all, while schools have succeeded in indoctrinating a portion of Mexican American youth in "success" values, they have not socialized them to a comparable extent in mobility-inducing behavior. Thus Mexican American children usually receive lower grades than Anglo American children and often feel embarrassed about it.[1] High school students frequently refer to their difficulties with subject matter taught in school, and even those who manage to enter college speak of such difficulties. I. Q. scores and school marks are generally regarded as valid indicators of behavior conducive to mobility, and Mexican American high school seniors rank far below their Anglo American peers in such behavior, even when socioeconomic class is held constant.[2]

A kind of self-fulfilling prophecy may be operating in the case of the Mexican American children's failure to develop necessary capacities and skills for advancement in school.[3] If the I. Q. scores of these children, as compared with those of Anglo Americans, were treated as indicators of initial disadvantages in terms of orientation and skills necessary for effective functioning in our society, then school programs probably could be designed to overcome these initial differences. But teachers tend to approach these scores as signs of fixed limits in innate ability.

Left to their own resources, these children are at a marked disadvantage in comparison with Anglo American pupils. Their parents, usually very limited in their own formal education, can seldom help them with their school work. Boys who have ambitious aspirations rarely discuss their plans with their fathers, as they regard their fathers' experiences irrelevant to their own problems: "I can't talk about this to my father," "it's no use," "our fathers don't talk to us," were persistent refrains in our interviews with Mexican American boys. This failure in communication fits into the patterns of the father-adolescent son conflict discussed in Chapter Three.[4]

Recent research regarding the effects of parental relationships suggests that boys with high scholastic achievement tend to be members of "equalitarian" households, while those with low achievement frequently come from wife-dominated homes.[5] No comparable information exists concerning the achievement of Mexican American boys. (One should note that equalitarian households appear to be a rarity among Mexican Americans.) Of possible relevance to this research, however, is one study which tested the hypothesis that Mexican American boys who are "achievers," in terms of high school grades, come from homes in which mothers are more dominating than they are in the homes of "underachievers." The achievers and non-achievers were matched on the basis of I. Q. scores, age, and school grades. Contrary to the investigators' expectations, the results show that the mothers of achieving boys are less dominating than the mothers of non-achievers.[6] This finding suggests that, in a "masculine" cultural environment such as the Mexican American, wife domination may have negative effects on the academic achievement of boys.[7]

Success Models

Clearly, few fathers of these boys can serve as models for their sons who have adopted conventional American goals and values of success. Other visible models, outside the home, are also scarce. Although there is little intergenerational rise in socioeconomic status, there are some Mexican Americans who have achieved considerable social, as well as economic, success—and the members of this small elite could have served as models *if* they were visible. But those Mexican Americans of superior achievement had a ready-made road to follow and thus spared themselves many of the hardships that descendants of most other foreign laborers and peasants had to undergo. For they were encouraged by the attitudes and behavior of the majority population to move out of the Mexican American community: they could pose as "Old Spanish" and find no important obstacles to acceptance in the higher strata of American society (providing, of course, that the marks of their Indian mixture were not too visible). Moreover, those persons of Mexican descent who have advanced substantially in the social scale have tended to sever their relations with the Mexican American community, thus perpetuating its lower class homogeneity.[8] As a Mexican American boy expresses it in Beatrice W. Griffith's book: "When a Negro starts going up, he hits the ceiling and can't go any further. But when a Mexican starts going up, he goes clear out of sight and becomes a good old Southern California family." [9]

This going "clear out of sight" probably accounts in large part for the absence of success models among Mexican Americans in the past. It may also throw some light on the fact that social mobility has long been synonymous with renunciation in the minds of many Mexican Americans.[10] "Has anybody in your neighborhood become successful?" I asked a Mexican

American college student. "Yes," he answered, "but he moved away and, as far as the boys are concerned, he is no longer Mexican."

It seems, however, that the pattern which led successful men to forsake their community is undergoing fundamental changes. A number of Mexican Americans who have achieved prominence in various fields during recent years have not severed but, on the contrary, have stressed their ties with the Mexican American community. Their very existence probably plays a part in the new mobility orientation of Mexican American youth. In contrast to the past, the high school boy can now answer the jeers of gang members that a Mexican is a fool to try because he will never make it, by pointing to those who did make it. But further study would be necessary to determine the extent to which Mexican American youngsters are consciously aware of successful individuals and the degree to which they have become models of emulation.

I found general agreement among college graduates of Mexican descent and among the educators and social workers who came into contact with Mexican Americans that the real breakthrough in the pattern of Mexican American nonmobility was made after World War II by the returning G. I.'s. When many of them began to enroll in college, these former servicemen were referred to as *locos,* crazy. The boys who today decide to go to college are less likely to be derided, for not only have a number of Mexican Americans completed college, but some of them have pursued graduate studies and entered the professions (especially teaching and social work, in which Mexicans are needed and sought). As one junior college student explained recently when telling about the *cholos'* attitudes toward college boys:

Some of them even envy you. That's what I noticed. Like Freddy has been kicked out of school but he is always going back to different schools. He is going now to a school that is miles away from his house. When he sees you, he says "You're going to college. That's wonderful." If they know you and see you they will always say hello. They have respect for you.

Today the Mexican American boy who is mobility-oriented is more apt to have a relative in his immediate or extended family who has attended college. The latter not only provides visibility, which is an important factor in the development of new patterns of behavior in the boy to whom he serves as a model, but he may also give the novice some practical hints which serve him well in this strange new world of opportunity.

One seldom reads about the kind of difficulties which spring from being disoriented in the ambiance of the larger society, but they become apparent in conversations and reminiscences of those who were able to overcome them. One of these young men, an ex-G.I., at a special conference devoted to the encouragement of higher education among Mexican Americans, remarked:

Some place along the line I met a friend who said, "Why don't you go to school?" "School? For me? What's that?" At that time I had a job in a small business; I was an auto mechanic. My partner sold the business, so I had time on my hands, and I came to this college. I walked in blind and looked around. I couldn't tell the difference between the teachers and the students. I remember I walked up to a student and I said, "What do I do?" He said, "I haven't time for you; ask one of the teachers." That dismayed me, so I went home. I came back the next day and met the same problem again. I remember I walked up to a psychology teacher, and I asked her, "What do I have to do to enroll?" She looked over some of the papers that I had, you know, the bundle of complicated forms they give you and she said, "You haven't even filled out your program?" "Program? What's that?" "You're supposed to take a number of units." "Units? What's units?" Well, eventually I caught on. I finally graduated from this school and I went on to UCLA.[11]

The ability to deal with such obstacles—trifling though they may appear to people not confronted by such handicaps—may make the difference between a college education or its rejection by the Mexican American boy or girl.

Now, achievement in any realm depends on at least three factors: that access to the field be open; that motivation for reaching the goal be present; and that the necessary resources, such as ability and "know-how" for reaching the goal, exist. These factors are of course interrelated. For example, the degree to which the realm is open to members of a given population will have a bearing on how widespread among them is the motivation to enter this particular area. On the other hand, a strong desire to reach the goal might force open doors that have been closed before.

Opportunities

The last two factors, motivation and resources, have already been explored. What about the extent of opportunities open to Mexican Americans? Treatment of this subject requires, of course, at least some consideration of problems associated with prejudice and discrimination. It is hard to imagine a Mexican American who has not experienced prejudice or discrimination in one form or another, even if only to hear himself or his people designated by the derogatory terms, such as "beans" or "greasers," that still abound in the Southwest. According to recent studies, these barriers may be weakening, but they continue to be widespread enough to afford little chance for a Mexican American to escape them altogether.[12]

The nature and extent of prejudice and discrimination against Mexican Americans are suggested in several studies. On the optimistic side, one investigation indicates that fewer younger people than older adults affirm prejudiced attitudes toward Mexican Americans —this may imply some hope for the future. This study also contrasts the attitudes of nonminority persons toward Mexican Americans and Negro Americans, noting that in the latter case the age of prejudiced persons appears to make little difference—and this too implies a less handicapped time ahead for Mexican Americans than for Negroes. Attitudes toward these two groups were studied in Bakersfield, California, where it was found in addition that there is considerably more sentiment in favor of integration with Mexican Americans than with Negroes. When asked the question "On the whole, would you like or dislike Mexican people?" only six percent of the Anglo American respondents answered in the negative (while 21 percent expressed a dislike for Negroes). But these respondents showed much less good will when asked more specific questions regarding their attitudes toward living in mixed neighborhoods with Mexican Americans, social intercourse, joint membership in clubs, and equality of treatment in employment; their strongest disapproval concerned integrated neighborhoods, and they had least objection to nondiscriminatory employment practices—only 38 percent of the respondents stated that Mexicans should "have the right to live with other Americans," whereas 83 percent maintained that Mexicans should have the right to "work side-by-side on the same jobs as other Americans." [13] These findings are consistent with those of another study, conducted in Tucson, Arizona, which also indicates that members of the majority population are more willing to accept Mexican Americans in the economic sphere than as neighborhood residents.[14] These various research studies, which document the continuing unwillingness of the dominant group to accept Mexican Americans as neighbors, help to explain the spatial isolation of Mexican Americans described in Chapter Two.

The studies of attitudes of prejudice, except by risky inference, give us no information about the extent of actual occupational opportunities open to Mexican Americans. To the best of our knowledge, there are no recent investigations of this specific question. Moreover, findings which bear on this question lack the consistency of the attitudinal studies. For example, a report on geographic subareas of Los Angeles concludes that "the occupation-and-income levels" of Mexican Americans "are relatively high in view of their limited educational attainment." [15] The investigation conducted in Racine, Wisconsin, cited earlier, on the other hand, gives a contrasting conclusion: occupationally, Mexican Americans in this community fare worse than Anglo Americans, even when the factor of education is controlled. A careful analysis of the relationship of education to the occupational level of the Mexican Americans in the Racine study resulted, according to the authors, "in most discouraging findings"—differences in their occupation levels and the majority population increased with schooling, and the gap was greater for those with a high school and college education than for those with less schooling.[16] These results suggest that the occupational opportunities for Mexican Americans are not uniform throughout the nation, including perhaps the Southwest itself.

Unequal opportunities should not obscure another fact—the evidence that Mexican Americans often lack the training to take advantage of some of the existing opportunities in such fields as teaching, social work, and public health.[17] For example, the Los Angeles

County Probation Department and social work agencies have for a number of years been stressing the need for, and their readiness to employ, Mexican Americans in these professions. Yet the number of Mexican Americans found in such positions is still disproportionately low.

Clearly, factors in addition to limited opportunities and prejudice help to determine the varying mobility rates of ethnic groups. One such factor, which is often disregarded in sociological studies, is the subjective approach of different groups to these limitations. Thus, in the case of Mexican Americans (as in other cases), one must not only ascertain to what extent opportunities were or are closed to them, but also how they have perceived and dealt with this situation. As early as 1929, Paul S. Taylor commented on the specific reaction of Mexican Americans to prejudice and discrimination:

> The Mexicans in the valley [San Joaquin, California] are sensitive to the social ostracism which they face, and do not force themselves in where they feel pressure against them. For instance, in some cases where tract salesmen sold to Mexicans, contrary to the desires of the company, they readily allowed themselves to be bought out . . . real estate men state that Mexicans do not seek to buy into non-Mexican neighborhoods in any under-cover ways. This *proud sensitiveness* was repeatedly revealed in various ways to the writer during conversations with Mexicans.[18] [italics supplied]

Significantly, from a study conducted about thirty years later, we learn that this "proud sensitiveness" is still the prevailing reaction of Mexican Americans to manifestation of ethnic prejudice. Thus real estate agents in San Antonio, Texas, report "that if something arises in the selling situation to disturb [Mexican Americans], to suggest that they are unfairly treated, to offend them, they will silently withdraw from the negotiations, despite their interest in buying a house." [19]

"Withdrawal," in a psychologically consistent manner, is also widely used by Mexican Americans as a solution to problems they face at work. They do not seem to be more alienated from work than Anglo Americans, according to a recent study of bank employees in Nogales, Arizona.[20] However, when they are or consider themselves to be deceived, cheated, or otherwise wronged by an employer, frequently they quit the job. In this way, a subjective cultural trait influences the frequently reported objective pattern of large numbers of both Mexican American factory and agricultural workers shifting from one job to another.[21]

Mexican Americans, generally, would rather not try to reach a goal barred by serious obstacles than pursue a goal at the risk of failure. Not to try does not reflect negatively on their manliness and honor but to try and fail does. Thus Mexican American culture provides the rationalization for staying out of the "failure region," to use Kurt Lewin's concept.[22] For example, the Los Angeles study shows that even among the mobility-oriented high school seniors, a significantly larger proportion of Mexican American than Anglo American boys (again, with class held constant) expressed preference for being a person who "tries to be satisfied with what he has" rather than someone "who is always looking for something better than he has." Similarly in the Racine study, more Mexican Americans than either Anglo Americans or Negroes held that "one must be content with what comes his way." [23]

It is pertinent to note that Mexican Americans do not have nation-wide organizations dedicated to the promotion and defense of their interests, comparable to Negro organizations such as the NAACP. They seldom assert themselves politically in organized political action. (One such rare occurrence was the successful campaign which brought about the election in 1957 of the first mayor of Mexican descent in the history of El Paso, a city whose population is almost half Mexican American.)[24] The Mexican American voluntary organizations tend to be more in the nature of social clubs. The few that do engage in action programs— like the previously mentioned LULAC (League of United Latin American Citizens), the Latin American Educational Foundation in Denver, or the Mexican American Education Committee in Los Angeles—tend to focus on encouraging the youth to finish high school and to aspire to higher education.[25]

As for the youth in particular, they seem fully in accord with the above pattern. My depth interviews of mobility-oriented Mexican American boys in Los Angeles during the summer of 1965 (which I terminated only one week before the Negro riots in the Watts section of town), suggest that Mexican Americans do not identify with the Negro struggle. Of the eighteen boys (ages 17 to 20), many were in favor of extending opportunities to all, including Negroes, but not one approved of the tactics used by them. They were especially vehement in their disapproval of demonstrations and sit-ins and definite in their rejection of their possible use by Mexican Americans. Here is an illustration, an excerpt from an interview with a 20-year-old.

(He) Before the Negroes started these sit-ins there was no trouble. We used to go into any section and be served but now with the demonstrations everything is jumpy. I find the sit-ins disgusting. Other people say that without the sit-ins the rights would not be recognized but I feel that at the present time the rights are highly recognized. In some states they are not, Negroes can't register. But why come here and demonstrate? Let them demonstrate there or go to Washing-

Conclusion

The material presented in this chapter and in Chapter Six indicates that ambitious and mobility-oriented young Mexican Americans are indeed handicapped as compared with their Anglo American peers. In most cases, they are born into larger families, their family training includes little emphasis on mobility values and behavior conducive to advancement, they acquire few such skills in school, their youthful world lacks visible models of achievement, they are not well aware of existing opportunities. Moreover, their ethnic identification and sense of group loyalty, however praiseworthy on other grounds, encourage behavior in keeping with traditional values and norms—and these may hamper mobility. The values of masculinity, honor, politeness, and leisure and the modes of conduct consistent with these values are a rationally unnecessary and heavy baggage on the road to conventional advancement, although they are cultural and psychological assets for those securely established at or near the top of the social pyramid.

However ambitious they may be, most mobility-oriented Mexican American young people cannot surmount these difficulties unaided. An open society, which professes a strong interest in opportunity for the members of all groups, requires effective mechanisms for overcoming historically and culturally rooted deficiencies in "capacities" and skills essential for advancement, as well as the mechanisms for instilling mobility consciousness and for strengthening achievement motivation.

We have seen that a new trend is developing among Mexican American youth. Contrary to the views held by many people, this trend strongly suggests that Mexican Americans do not constitute an exception to the characteristic historical pattern of minority ethnic groups in the United States whereby many of their members have realized, at least in some measure, the goals of the American Dream. The process observed in other groups is being similarly reenacted here, although it took a few more generations to initiate it. Only now is its emergence sufficiently visible to justify naming it a "trend." Whether this long-delayed trend will be halted or hastened depends largely upon our society's deliberate removal of the obstacles that continue to block the advancement of these ambitious Americans, the new and staunch converts to the American Dream.

Notes

1. Clark, *op. cit.*, p. 68.

2. Heller, "Ambitions of Mexican-American Youth . . . ," *op. cit.*, pp. 143-85.

3. Robert K. Merton, "The Self-Fulfilling Prophecy," in *Social Theory and Social Structure*, Glencoe: The Free Press, 1957, pp. 421-34.

4. De Hoyos also found that the communication between parents and teen-age sons, whom he studied, was rather poor. See: De Hoyos, *op. cit.*, p. 119.

5. Glen H. Elder, Jr., "Family Structure and Educational Attainment: A Cross-National Analysis," *American Sociological Review*, 30 (February, 1965), p. 83.

6. Achievers were defined as those whose grades were above the seventieth percentile of their class and underachievers as those below the thirtieth percentile. See: Louis J. Gill and Bernard Spilka, "Some Nonintellectual Correlates of Academic Achievement among Mexican-American Secondary School Students," *Journal of Educational Psychology*, 53 (June, 1962), pp. 145-7.

7. Elder, *op. cit.*, pp. 83-4.

8. Broom and Shevky, *op. cit.*, p. 156.

9. Griffith, *op. cit.*, pp. 229-30.

10. McWilliams, *op. cit.*, p. 37.

11. *Proceedings*, Conference on the Education of Spanish-Speaking People, *op. cit.*, pp. 36-7.

12. Robin M. Williams, *Strangers Next Door*, Englewood Cliffs, N. J.: Prentice-Hall, 1964, p. 65.

13. Alphonso Pinkney, "Prejudice toward Mexican and Negro Americans: A Comparison," *Phylon* (First Quarter, 1963), pp. 355, 357-8.

14. Raymond A. Mulligan, "Socioeconomic Background and Minority Attitudes," *Sociology and Social Research*, 45 (April, 1961), pp. 289-95.

15. *Background for Planning, op. cit.*, p. 62.

16. Lyle W. Shannon and Elaine Krass, "The Urban Adjustment of Immigrants: The Relationship of Education to Occupation and Total Family Income," *Pacific Sociological Review*, 6 (Spring, 1963), pp. 137-42.

17. William V. D'Antonio and Julian Samora, "Occupational Stratification in Four Southwestern Communities," *Social Forces* (October, 1962), p. 25; Burma, *op. cit.*, p. 132.

18. Taylor, *op. cit.*, pp. 81-2.

19. Dodson, *op. cit.*, p. 96.

20. Louis A. Zurcher, Arnold Meadow, and Susan Lee Zurcher, "Value Orientation, Role Conflict, and Alienation from Work: A Cross-Cultural Study," *American Sociological Review*, 30 (August, 1965), p. 544.

21. See, e.g.: Octavio Romano, "Donship in a Mexican-American Community in Texas," *American Anthropologist*, 62 (December, 1960), p. 973.

22. Kurt Lewin, T. Dembo, L. Festinger, and P. Sears, "Level of Aspiration," in J. McV. Hunt, ed., *Personality and Behavior Disorders*, Vol. 1, New York: Ronald Press, 1944, p. 375.

23. Heller, "Ambitions of Mexican-American Youth . . . ," *op. cit.*, p. 227; Shannon and Krass, "The Economic Absorption and Cultural Integration of Inmigrant Mexican-American and Negro Workers," *op. cit.*, p. 202.

24. William V. D'Antonio and William H. Form, *Influentials in Two Border Cities—A Study in Community Decision*, Notre Dame: University of Notre Dame Press, 1965, pp. 125-44.

25. *Ibid.*, p. 246; Christian, *op. cit.*, p. 38.

26. *Proceedings*, Conference on Educational Problems of Students of Mexican Descent, *op. cit.*, pp. 2-3.

27. D'Antonio and Samora, *op. cit.*, pp. 17-25.

28. Clark, *op. cit.*, p. 31.

29. Tuck, *op. cit.*, p. 189-90.

Recommended Readings

Barker, George C., *Pachuco, An American-Spanish Argot and Its Social Functions in Tucson, Arizona.* Tucson: University of Arizona Press, January, 1950, Social Science Bulletin, 21, No. 18.

A *linguistic study of the distinct vocabulary and idioms of members of delinquent gangs.*

Broom, Leonard, and Shevky, Eshref, "Mexicans in the United States—A Problem in Social Differentiation." *Sociology and Social Research,* 36 (January-February, 1952), pp. 150-58.

A *sociological analysis of the relative lack of internal differentiation in the Mexican American minority group.*

Clark, Margaret, *Health in the Mexican-American Culture, A Community Study.* Berkeley: University of California Press, 1959.

An *ethnographic study of the Mexican American community in San Jose, California.*

D'Antonio, William V., and Samora, Julian, "Occupational Stratification in Four Southwestern Communities." *Social Forces* (October, 1962), pp. 17-25.

A *study of the distribution of Mexican Americans in public health occupations.*

Edmonson, Munroe, *Los Manitos—A Study of Institutional Values*. New Orleans: Middle American Research Institute, Tulane University, 1957.
An anthropological study of the basic values of Mexican Americans in New Mexico.

Gamio, Manuel, *Mexican Immigration to the United States: A Study of Human Migration and Adjustment*. Chicago: University of Chicago Press, 1930.
The classic scholarly work about Mexican immigrants.

Griffith, Beatrice, *American Me*. Boston: Houghton Mifflin Co., 1948.
A sympathetic and unusually insightful treatment of Mexican boys and girls who are marked as juvenile delinquents.

Kluckhohn, Florence R., "The Spanish-Americans of Atrisco" in Florence R. Kluckhohn and Fred L. Strodtbeck, *Variations in Value Orientations*. New York: Row, Peterson & Co., 1961, pp. 175-257.
A study of changes in the value orientations of Mexican Americans in a small rural community of New Mexico.

Pinkney, Alphonso, "Prejudice toward Mexican and Negro Americans." *Phylon* (First Quarter, 1963), pp. 353-9.
Part of the Cornell studies in intergroup relations.

Rose, Peter I., *They and We*. New York: Random House, 1964.
A concise general treatment of ethnic groups in the United States.

Sanchez, George, *Forgotten People*. Albuquerque: University of New Mexico Press, 1940.
An educator's penetrating analysis of the mode of life and problems of Mexican Americans in New Mexico.

Taylor, Paul S., "Mexican Labor in the United States." University of California Publications in Economics, Vol. VI. Berkeley: University of California Press, 1929, pp. 257-92.
An economist's thorough description of the economic and living conditions of Mexican American agricultural workers in California in the 1920s.

Tuck, Ruth, *Not with the Fist*. New York: Harcourt, Brace & Co., 1946.
A well-known anthropological study of a Mexican American community in California.

Turner, Ralph H., and Surace, Samuel J., "Zoot-suiters and Mexicans: Symbols in Crowd Behavior." *American Journal of Sociology*, 62 (July, 1956), pp. 14-20.
A social psychological analysis of the factors operating in the 1943 Los Angeles riots against Mexican Americans.

Index